FAIRY TALE FEASTS

A LITERARY COOKBOOK
FOR YOUNG READERS AND EATERS

This paperback edition published in 2014 by

CROCODILE BOOKS

An imprint of Interlink Publishing Group, Inc.

46 Crosby Street, Northampton, Massachusetts 01060

www.interlinkbooks.com

Library of Congress Cataloging-in-Publication Data

Yolen, Jane.

Fairy tale feasts : a literary cookbook for young readers and eaters / by Jane Yolen and Heidi E.Y. Stemple ; illustrations by Philippe Béha.—1st ed.

p. cm.

ISBN 1-56656-643-6 (hardback : alk. paper)

1. Cookery—Juvenile literature. I. Stemple, Heidi E. Y. II. Béha, Philippe. III. Title.

TX652.5.Y65 2006

641.5'123—dc22

2005036047

ISBN 10: 1-56656-643-6

ISBN 13: 978-1-56656-643-8

ISBN 13: 978-1-56656-751-0

This book was typeset in Black Beard and Baskerville Book.

Book and jacket design by Elisa Gutiérrez

Chapter graphics by Elisa Gutiérrez

Additional design and layout by Jacqueline Wang and Juliana Spear

Printed and bound in China

10 9 8 7 6 5 4 3

FAIRY TALE FEASTS

A LITERARY COOKBOOK FOR YOUNG READERS AND EATERS

Fairy Tales retold by

Jane Yolen

Recipes by

Heidi E.Y. Stemple

Illustrations by

Phillipe Béha

Crocodile Books, USA

An imprint of Interlink Publishing Group, Inc.

www.interlinkbooks.com

For my daughter, for meals cooked, jokes shared, and love always
—JY

For Jen and the thousands of dinners we cooked together, for Nina whose name should be on this book for all the help she gave me, and for all my taste testers especially my daughters—Maddison and Glendon
—HEYS

For my daughters Sara and Fanny
—PB

A story is not beautiful unless something is added to it.
—*Tuscan proverb*

CONTENTS

Stories and Stovetops: An Introduction

From the earliest days of stories, when hunters came home from the hunt to tell of their exploits around the campfire while gnawing on a leg of beast, to the era of kings in castles listening to the storyteller at the royal dinner feast, to the time of TV dinners when whole families gathered to eat and watch movies together, stories and eating have been close companions.

So it is not unusual that folk stories are often about food: Jack's milk cow traded for beans, Snow White given a poisoned apple, a pancake running away from those who would eat it.

But there is something more—and this is about the powerful ties between stories and recipes. Both are changeable, suiting the need of the maker and the consumer.

A storyteller never tells the same story twice, because every audience needs a slightly different story, depending upon the season or the time of day, the restlessness of the youngest listener, or how appropriate a tale is to what has just happened in the storyteller's world. And every cook knows that a recipe changes according to the time of day, the weather, the altitude, the number of grains in the level teaspoonful, the ingredients found (or not found) in the cupboard or refrigerator, the tastes or allergies of the dinner guests, even the cook's own feelings about the look of the batter.

So if you want to tell these stories yourself or make these recipes yourself, be playful. After first making them exactly as they are in this book, you can begin to experiment. Recipes, like stories, are made more beautiful by what *you* add to it. Add, subtract, change, try new ways. We have, and we expect you will, too. In fact, in the recipes, we have already given you some alternatives, like different toppings and other spices.

–Jane Yolen and Heidi E. Y. Stemple

A NOTE FROM THE STORYTELLER

All these stories are retold by me, but are based on old folktales—except for the last one, which I made up entirely. When a storyteller retells a folktale, she seeks out as many versions as possible, understands the story's structure, and then uses her own words in the telling.

In some cases I have added dialogue, description, or rhymes. Occasionally I have renamed characters. I always look for new ways to say old things. And as I work, I always read the stories aloud to make sure they trip easily off the tongue.

Finally there are marginalia—notes set in the margins of the stories—to tell you where each story comes from and how it has traveled. When I talk about a "tale type" I am referring to the Aarne-Thompson Index, also called "The Types of the Folktale." It is a system of grouping stories (mostly European tales) by reference numbers according to their themes and was first developed in 1910 by Finnish folklorist Antti Aarne. That system was later enlarged by American folklorist Stith Thompson in 1928, then updated again in 1961. The volumes in "The Types of the Folktale" help folktale researchers see which stories share common themes or building-block incidents.

—JANE YOLEN

A NOTE FROM THE COOK

The recipes in this book were put together by me. I am not a professional chef, just a mom who enjoys cooking with her children. Some of these recipes I cook all the time (Lemon Chicken and the Seaweed Stuffed Shells are family favorites.) Some were gifts from particularly generous friends. And some were created especially for this book. But, for each one, I cooked many different batches, re-measuring and changing ingredients, trying to make them both delicious and easy to understand.

As with all recipes, you have to make allowances for differences in equipment, ingredients available locally and seasonally. Some recipes are difficult and will require a grownup's help and a special trip to the grocery store. Others will require only what is already in your kitchen.

But cooking should not only be about the end product. Like a story, it's about the act of creating as well.

My main chef's helpers—and taste testers—were Maddison Jane, age 7, and Glendon, age 19. They are now 11 and 23. Recipes can be made in a short time. Books take a lot longer. My children, being so different in age, help me cook in different ways. Maddison enjoys stirring, cracking eggs, and measuring, while I have Glendon do prep work, such as cutting of vegetables and meats. They both enjoy the eating.

When making the recipes in this book, make sure to have parental supervision using knives or cooking. That way, each parent can decide what each young chef is capable of. Always remember safety in the kitchen—the obvious dangers are heat and knives. But also remember to pull back long hair, especially if you are cooking on a gas stove. Wash your hands and equipment often and keep the ingredients you are going to eat raw away from foods you are preparing to cook, especially raw meat.

Now, pick out your recipe and set out your equipment. Gather your ingredients and start cooking!

—HEIDI E. Y. STEMPLE

11

BREAKFASTS

THE MAGIC POT OF PORRIDGE
Perfect Porridge

THE BREWERY OF EGGSHELLS
Eggs in a Cradle

DIAMONDS AND TOADS
Very French Toast

THE RUNAWAY PANCAKE
Runaway Pancakes

THE MAGIC POT OF PORRIDGE

There was once a poor but good girl named Grete, who lived all alone with her mother by the side of a great forest. Times had been hard and there was nothing left in their cupboards to eat, so Grete decided on her own to go into the forest to look for food.

As she was wandering through the deep woods, she met an old woman who seemed to know exactly what was the matter.

"You are hungry, child?"

Grete curtsied and nodded. "I am hungry, good frau. But not as hungry as my dear mother."

The old fairy—for, of course, she was such—smiled and handed Grete a pot, saying "Take this and instruct it, 'Cook, little pot, cook.' It will give you as much sweet porridge as you and your mother can eat. And when you are full, tell it, 'Stop, little pot, stop.' And it will immediately cease to cook."

Grete took the pot and gazed down into its shiny surface. When she looked up again to thank the old woman, she had vanished.

Published by the Brothers Grimm as "Sweet Porridge," this story is part of a whole group of tales known as "magic pot" stories. It is filed in the famous Aarne-Thompson tale type index as type 565. Companion tales to this are the Norwegian "Mill That Grinds Salt at the Bottom of the Sea," and all the Sorcerer's Apprentice stories.

Now Grete knew better than to shrug off a fairy's blessing, so she took the pot right home to her mother. She set the pot on the stove and said the magic words and the pot cooked them sweet porridge until they could eat no more.

The next morning Grete went out again into the forest, to try and find the old woman to thank her, leaving the pot at home with her mother.

Now her mother was feeling a bit peckish—which is to say, hunger pangs pecked at her belly again. So she turned to the pot on the stove and said—as her daughter had, "Cook, little pot, cook."

At once the little pot cooked up some wonderful sweet porridge and the mother soon ate her fill. But she hadn't listened carefully to her daughter's instructions on how to stop the pot, and so she cried out, "Enough!"

The pot did not listen, of course, and keep cooking merrily away.

Then the mother began to cry out everything she could think of—"Cease, pot! Enough! Stop cooking! That's plenty! Help!"

But the pot kept cooking more and more porridge.

The porridge filled the pot, rose over the edge, spilled onto the stove, over onto the floor.

"Stop it, pot!" the frantic mother cried. "That's too much! Oh dear, oh dear, oh dear!"

The pot kept cooking.

Porridge filled up the kitchen and then the house, went along the lane to the next house, filled *it* up with porridge and then continued on down the street.

The mother ran out crying for help.

The people in the next house went crying for help.

The people in the village went crying for help.

Finally little Grete came home from the forest and realized what had happened.

"Stop, little pot, stop!" she called.

The pot stopped cooking.

And everyone who wanted to go home had to eat their way back.

The grinding mill tale has been found in various tellings from Norway, all the way through Central Europe and down into Greece. It made its way to America, China, and Japan. The famous children's book writer and illustrator Tomie dePaola did his own version, Strega Nona, *which he set in Italy with a magic pasta pot and a silly hero named Big Anthony.*

Perfect Porridge

So good, you'll want more than one bowl. (Makes an individual serving)

 EQUIPMENT:

- measuring cup
- pan
- wooden spoon

 INGREDIENTS:

- 1 cup water (230 ml)
- ½ cup oats (40 g)
- dash salt

DIRECTIONS:

1. For each large serving, pour 1 cup of water and a dash of salt into the pan over high heat and bring to a boil.

2. Once water boils, pour in the oats.

3. Turn heat down to medium-high, and stir for 5 minutes, to keep from having lumpy porridge.

4. Serve with salt and milk like the Scots do, or with your favorite toppings (see variations).

NOTE:

For each additional serving, use another cup (230 ml) of water and cup (40 g) of oats.

Facts about porridge:
1. Porridge is another word for oatmeal, which is made of boiled oats. Children throughout Europe, both rich and poor, ate it for breakfast, but rich children had sugar and cream with their porridge. Poor children ate it with skimmed milk (milk with the cream skimmed off the top) and treacle, a kind of molasses.
2. In the old days, porridge was eaten with a wooden spoon, because metal spoons became too hot. The favorite wood for a porridge spoon was birch because it was so easy to keep clean.

VARIATIONS:

Many Americans (and probably Scots, too) like a sweeter porridge.

1. Maple and Brown Sugar: Top with 1 tablespoon maple syrup, 1 tablespoon brown sugar and a dollop of milk or cream.

2. Butter and Brown Sugar: Top with 1 tablespoon butter and 1 tablespoon brown sugar and a dollop of milk or cream.

3. Bananas and Cream: Mash half a banana with a fork in your bowl. Add 1 tablespoon milk or cream. Add to hot porridge.

4. Apples and Cinnamon: Cut half an apple into small cubes and add to the boiling water with the oats. When cooked, add a tablespoon sugar and ¼ teaspoon cinnamon. Top with a dollop of cream or milk.

5. Raisins and Spice: Add a heaping tablespoon raisins to cooking oats. When cooked, add ¼ teaspoon cinnamon and a dash of ground nutmeg. Top with a dollop of cream or milk.

6. Holiday Porridge: Mix together ¼ cup (60 ml) eggnog with a dash of cinnamon, nutmeg, and cloves. Add to cooked porridge.

3. Scottish porridge makers use a "spurtle," a little wooden stick, to stir their porridge. They always stir it to the right, not the left, which is considered bad luck.
4. Scottish soldiers often carried little bags of oats with them for a hearty hot meal that could be cooked quickly in boiling water over a campfire.

THE BREWERY OF EGGSHELLS

Once not so long ago, a certain Eileen Murphy gave birth to a baby boy she named Tam. He was a big, healthy, smiling child with bright blue eyes, and a dimple in his chin. At least he was that way on Saturday night when she tucked him into his cradle.

On Sunday morning, before church, he had become a shriveled, squalling, scrawny infant.

"Heavens preserve us!" cried Mrs. Murphy, "the Good Folk have come and exchanged one of theirs for mine, for surely that is a changeling child and not my Tam."

Her friends told her what to do, for it was well known how to treat an imp. "Roast it on a griddle," said one. "Grab its nose with hot iron tongs," said another. "Throw it in the snow," said a third.

But she could not bear to treat the changeling badly. It was a baby, after all, even though it was a devilish child who cried from morning to night and would not be comforted.

So it went for ten days until Mrs. Murphy and her husband were fair exhausted by the babe. And then, as luck would have it—good, bad, and otherwise—Grey Ellen came calling.

Now Grey Ellen was a wise woman of the kind rarely seen today. She knew all the fairy lore, not just a smattering, and had what is called the "gift." She wandered the countryside, going door to door, helping folk who needed it and even those who did not. Nowadays we would call her a beggar and shoo her away, but then she was fed for a blessing, and given shelter for her wisdom.

"Good day to you, Eileen Murphy," said Grey Ellen.

"Good day it may be," replied Mrs. Murphy, "but for the changeling child who lies in my own Tam's cradle." As she spoke, the changeling set up an awful wail, high as a rabbit's scream.

"Ah," said Grey Ellen, putting a finger aside her nose. "And you cannot bring yourself to roast it or toast it or grab its nose with tongs."

Mrs. Murphy shook her head.

"And this being a summer's day, there's no snow in which to toss it."

Mrs. Murphy nodded her head.

"Then I know just the thing," said Grey Ellen. "Just do as I bid you, and all will be well."

"You will not hurt the poor thing?" asked Mrs. Murphy, her heart full of fear.

Grey Ellen smiled. "I will not, for is it not a child of the Fair

Folk? But this is what you must do." And she told her.

Mrs. Murphy gave Grey Ellen a fine tea, with three different kinds of cakes in thanks. Then off went Grey Ellen to help someone else, and into the nursery went Mrs. Murphy.

She brought the child out into the main room of the cottage and laid the baby in a basket by the fire. Then she put a big pot of water on to boil.

The changeling followed her with its big, dark eyes.

Next Mrs. Murphy got out a dozen new-laid eggs, broke them, threw away the insides, and put the shells into the boiling water.

"Yum. . ." she said, "and don't these eggshells smell fine."

Now the baby had been quietly watching everything with great interest for about a quarter of an hour. Suddenly it opened its mouth. But instead of wailing, it said in an old man's voice,

Although this is the Irish version, the method of discovering a changeling child by brewing a meal in an eggshell is popular throughout Europe. In Germany, a similar tale tells how the brewery made the changeling laugh. In the Danish story, a pudding made of pig's hide and hair is cooked instead of eggshells. The point of the story is always that the odd meal forces the changeling to respond and is thus found out. This story is so popular, it has its own motif number: F321.1

"What are you doing, Mommy?"

Mrs. Murphy nearly died of fright that a ten-day-old child should speak, but she answered as Grey Ellen had advised her. "I'm brewing, my son."

"And what are you brewing, Mommy?" asked the child, sitting up in the basket. There was now no question it was a fairy, for surely no ten-day-old baby could do such a thing.

"Eggshells," said Mrs. Murphy. "I'm brewing eggshells."

"Oh!" cried the imp, clapping its tiny hands. "I'm a thousand years in this world and I never saw a brewery of eggshells before!" He leaped up out of the basket, turned around three times on the floor, and disappeared.

A tiny sound came from the basket. Mrs. Murphy ran over to look and there was her little Tam, all sweet-smelling and smiles, bright blue eyes and a dimple in his chin, looking up at her. And never again were the Murphys bothered by the fairies. ⭐

EGGS IN A CRADLE

Because you wouldn't want to eat eggshells for breakfast.

(Makes 3 servings)

EQUIPMENT:

- medium sized cup or glass
- butter knife
- spatula
- griddle (or large skillet)

INGREDIENTS:

- 3 eggs
- 3 pieces of bread
- butter (soft is best)
- salt and pepper
- sliced cheese (optional)

DIRECTIONS

1. Place each piece of bread on a flat surface and put the cup on top of it—upside down. If you cannot see the outside of the bread on all sides, the cup is too big.

2. Gently press the cup down, twisting a bit, to cut out a circle in the middle of each slice of bread. These are your egg cradles. Repeat on each slice of bread. Save the middle rounds for the birds or for eating later.

3. Butter both sides of the cradles. Hint: If your butter is hard from the refrigerator, it will break the bread. Better to melt enough butter in the pan to coat it instead.

4. Warm up the griddle to a medium heat. Place the cradles in it. Drop a small amount of butter into the hole of each (about ¼ tablespoon) unless you have buttered the whole pan.

5. Carefully crack an egg into each cradle.

6. Cook until firm on the cooking side and milky (no longer clear) on the side up.

7. Flip each piece. Hint: make sure to get the spatula under as much of the center egg section as possible or the egg may not hold together.

8. If you want, you may *tuck in* each egg with a slice of cheese.

9. Cook for only a minute or two so as not to overcook the yolk. If you wish to have a solid yolk, pierce it with a fork or the sharp edge of the eggshell as soon as you crack it into the bread in step 5.

10. Serve with salt and pepper.

4. When an egg is laid, it is warm.
5. Albumen is another name for the egg white. It contains 67 percent of the egg's liquid weight and half of its protein.
6. Eggs were not an important part of human diets until Roman times.

CHEESES AND BREADS:

Any bread will work for this recipe, but pre-sliced bread makes it much easier.

Experiment with your cheeses. American is fine, but try more adventurous cheeses such as cheddar, Colby, Monterey jack, or even a dill havarti.

VARIATIONS:

For a meatier breakfast, instead of or in addition to the cheese, try tucking in the egg with some ham or bacon strips.

SERVING HINT:

When serving a dish with salt and pepper, offer both at the table, but do not garnish the dish while cooking. Each eater should be able to salt and pepper their food according to their individual tastes and diets. 🍅

DIAMONDS AND TOADS

There was once a widow with two daughters. Now, the oldest daughter was like her mother: ugly and arrogant and mean. The youngest daughter was sweet and kind and lovely. She took after her dear, dead father.

Of course, the widow favored the older daughter, whom she called a gem, and hated the youngest. She gave her the nickname of Slop Girl and made her do all the kitchen work, and all the sweeping and fetching and carrying.

Now one day, in order to punish Slop Girl even more than usual, the widow called her over and said, "Our well is running dry. I want you to go deep into the forest where there is a clear stream and draw our water from that."

Slop Girl nodded.

"And as you will be gone all morning, you can carry a crust of *pain perdu*, day-old bread, with you."

Slop Girl nodded again, took the crust of bread gratefully, and put it in her apron pocket. She walked and walked for several hours before she found the stream. Sitting down on a rock, she began to eat her crust of bread so that she might have energy to draw out the water.

Just then she saw a poor old woman coming along the road, bent over a hawthorn staff.

The old woman sat down next to her and sighed. "I haven't eaten for days," she said.

Slop Girl held out the crust. "It's all I have, but you are welcome to it," she said. "And I will draw some water from the stream so you may drink as well." And she did so with such sweetness that the old woman smiled saying, "Kindness is always rewarded, child. The gift I shall give you is that every word you speak from now on will be accompanied by diamonds and pearls." And she was suddenly gone.

Slop Girl filled the pitcher again and hurried home where her mother scolded her for being late.

"I am so sorry. . ." Slop Girl began, and two diamonds and two pearls suddenly appeared with her words.

Her mother was so stunned by this, she encouraged Slop Girl to tell her the whole story, which was about a hundred and fifty more jewels.

No sooner had she understood the story, then the mother sent for her older daughter, the one upon whom she lavished all her love. She gave her a round of fresh bread and a tiny pitcher and sent her off into the woods, though the girl complained the entire way.

But when the old fairy (who else could it be?) came along, bent over a hawthorn stick, the older sister would give her neither a bit of the bread nor a drink from the pitcher. She said instead, "I am not your servant, old lady. So just give me my gift and be gone!"

The fairy nodded and her mouth twisted about. "A gift to suit you indeed," she said. "Every time you speak, your cruel and poisonous words will be accompanied by toads."

The older sister did not believe her until she got home. And then she started to say, "Mama, you would not believe how awful that old lady was. And how smelly!" Fourteen foul toads dropped from her mouth, some as small as pennies and some as big as apples.

Frightened, the widow ran off and her elder daughter after her, crying, "Mama, it's not my fault. . ."—which meant another five toads.

"You are right, my poor pet," cried the mother, "it's Slop Girl's fault." They turned back and beat the poor youngest sister black and blue, until she ran out of the house weeping.

There along the road came a handsome prince who fell in love with Slop Girl before she even spoke a word. And of course he loved her even more after. ★

This particular story comes from the Charles Perrault collection of fairy tales, compiled in 1697. Perrault was not writing for children. He was using folktales to talk about the nature of the French court of his day. An earlier version of the story had already appeared in the 1634 Italian collection, Pentamarone. About that old fairy— sometimes the reward-giver in the story is God accompanied by three angels.

33

Very French Toast

A gem of a breakfast. (Makes 3 servings)

EQUIPMENT:
- bowl
- fork
- measuring spoons
- griddle (or large skillet)
- spatula

INGREDIENTS:
- 6 slices of bread
- 4 eggs
- 1 tbsp. cream or milk
- 1 tsp. vanilla
- 1 tbsp. sugar
- ½ tsp. cinnamon
- ¼ tsp. nutmeg
- butter
- syrup (maple, strawberry, blueberry, raspberry—your choice)

Facts about French toast:

1. In France, French Toast is called pain perdu, *or "lost bread" because the bread is smothered or lost under many other ingredients.*

2. Other cooking experts say pain perdu *is a term that refers to the fact that French bread goes stale in a day or two and would be discarded or lost to use.*

3. In the south of France pain perdu *is eaten at Easter time as a part of the day's celebration.*

DIRECTIONS:

1. Crack the eggs into the bowl. Using the fork, beat the eggs.

2. Add cream and vanilla and beat together.

3. Add the sugar and spices and beat together.

4. Heat the griddle to a medium-high heat and melt approximately 2 tablespoons of butter—enough to coat the entire bottom. Cooking oil can be substituted here (approximately 1 tablespoon).

5. Dip each piece of bread into the egg mixture, coating both sides. You can use your fingers and the fork. Do this quickly so as not to soak in too much mixture, but make sure each piece is thoroughly coated.

6. Place dipped slices on the griddle and cook until golden brown.

7. Flip each piece with the spatula in the order you put them on.

8. When the French toast is golden brown on both sides, remove pieces (two to a plate) and serve with butter and syrup.

4. The British version of French Toast is called "poor knight's pudding" or the "poor knights of Windsor" because it is a cheap meal made by sandwiching jam or syrup between two slices of battered and browned bread. The Germans similarly call the dish arme Ritter, *or poor knights.*

5. The Dutch call this dish wentelteefjes. *The first part is from a word meaning "soaked." Teefje is an old word for a particular shape of pastry—and refers to a female dog.*

VARIATIONS:

Holiday French Toast: Substitute eggnog for the cream, and use ¼ teaspoon each of cinnamon, nutmeg, and ground cloves.

ALTERNATE TOPPINGS:

1. Fresh strawberries cut up and sprinkled with confectioner's sugar or topped with whipped cream makes a delicious and very fancy breakfast.

2. Peel and slice 3 apples and sauté them in ¾ cup (175 ml) cranberry juice for a unique topping.

BREAD:

Any type of bread may be used for French Toast—white, wheat, 7-grain, Italian. And the bread does not have to be fresh. In fact, using slightly stale bread is actually better.

Be creative in your selection of bread. How about trying cinnamon raisin bread, banana nut bread, or even zucchini bread? For fun shapes, cut the slices of bread with cookie cutters before dipping them in the egg mixture. 🍎

THE RUNAWAY PANCAKE

In old Norway there was once a housewife with seven hungry children: Ole, Rolle, Halvor, Mary, Kirsten, Karen, and Little Peter Gynt.

One day, as she was making pancakes for their meal, she used new milk instead of day-old. When she started frying the pancakes, one lay in the pan, beautiful and thick. The children watched her, and her good husband sat by the fire looking on.

"Oh, Mama, I am so hungry," cried Ole. "Give me a bit of the pancake in the pan."

"Ah, please, Mama," said Rolle.

"Please, dear Mama," said Halvor.

"Please dear darling Mama," said Mary.

"Please dear darling kind Mama," said Kirsten.

"Please dear darling kind and generous Mama," said Karen.

"Please dear darling kind and generous and sweet Mama," said Little Peter Gynt.

Mama sighed. "Wait until it turns itself," she said, though she meant to say, *until I have turned it.* But she was tired and frazzled and not speaking plain.

This popular Norwegian tale is one of many European versions. It has its own folklore number: type 2025, the fleeing pancake. The teller can add as many creatures along the way as needed: hen and cock, duck and gander, cow, horse, dog, cat—and always pig.
This kind of story is known as a cumulative tale, which simply means that the story winds up predictably one way and then snap! *It's over. Other popular cumulative stories are "The House That Jack Built" and "The Old Lady and Her Pig."*

The pancake heard this, was frightened and excited at once, and tried to climb out of the pan. However, it only turned itself on the other side, where it fried a bit more.

"Halloo," cried Ole, Rolle, Halvor, Mary, Kirsten, Karen, and Little Peter Gynt, "see what the pancake has done."

Mama came over to see, and at that, the pancake, feeling stronger than before, jumped out of the pan and onto the floor, rolling away just like a cart wheel, right through the open door and down the road.

Well, Mama ran after it, frying pan in one hand, ladle in the other. After her went Ole, Rolle, Halvor, Mary, Kirsten, Karen, and Little Peter Gynt, waving their napkins. And the good husband came running last of all, his cane in his hand. All of them shouted for the pancake to stop which only seemed to make it go faster. Soon it was so far ahead they could no longer see it, and they were so tired, they stopped, turned around, and went home.

But the pancake rolled on and on until it met a bearded man.

"Halloo, pancake," said the man, who was hungry.

"Halloo, Manny Panny," said the pancake.

"Wait a bit, pancake and I will eat you," said the hungry man.

"I have run way from Goody Poody and her old husband and her seven squalling children: Ole, Rolle, Halvor, Mary, Kirsten, Karen, and Little Peter Gynt and I shall run away from you, too."

Off rolled the pancake over the hill and out of sight.

The pancake rolled and rolled until it met a peckish hen.

"Halloo, pancake," said the hen.

"Halloo, Henny Penny," said the pancake.

"Don't roll so fast," said the peckish hen, "for I would love to peck you."

"I have run away from the hungry man, from Goody Poody and her old husband and her seven squalling children: Ole, Rolle, Halvor, Mary, Kirsten, Karen, and Little Peter Gynt. And I shall run away from you, too." Off rolled the pancake over the hill and out of sight.

The pancake rolled and rolled until it met a plucky duck.

In the Scottish version the main character is a bannock, *an oatmeal cake. In Russia, he is a talking bun. There are tales in Germany, Slovenia, and over thirty Irish versions. "The Gingerbread Man", an ever-popular American version of the story, was first published in St. Nicholas Magazine in May 1875. The refrain from the American version is still popular:*

Run, run
as fast as you can,
You can't catch me,
I'm the
Gingerbread Man.

"Halloo, pancake," said the duck.

"Halloo, Ducky Lucky," said the pancake.

"Don't roll so fast," said the plucky duck, "for I would love to pluck you."

"I have run way from the peckish hen, from a hungry man, from Goody Poody and her old husband and her seven squalling children: Ole, Rolle, Halvor, Mary, Kirsten, Karen, and Little Peter Gynt. And I shall run away from you, too." Off rolled the pancake over the hill and out of sight.

The pancake rolled and rolled until it met a portly pig standing near a dark and tangled wood.

"Halloo pancake," said the pig.

"Halloo Piggy Wiggy," said the pancake.

"Don't roll so fast," said the portly pig, "for I am a slow-goer. Let's walk a bit and talk a bit. You look like someone who has seen a lot of the world. If we keep company, we can keep one another safe."

Now the pancake was not, in fact, someone who had seen much of the world. And the woods did, indeed, look dark and dangerous. So he decided to travel with the portly pig until they came to a little river.

"I can swim over," said the pig, "and carry you on my back. Otherwise you will get all wet and fall to pieces."

So the pancake climbed upon the pig's back. But when they were in the middle of the water, the pig looked over his shoulder and *Snip-Snap!* He ate up the pancake in one easy bite. Which is the end of the story. And the end of the pancake as well! ⭐

Runaway Pancakes

Eat them quick before they get away. (Makes 2–4 servings)

EQUIPMENT:

- measuring spoons
- large measuring cup (or medium-sized bowl)
- large spoon or whisk
- large mixing bowl
- large skillet or electric skillet with a top
- spatula

INGREDIENTS:

- 1 cup flour (115 g)
- 1 tbsp. sugar
- 1 tbsp. baking powder
- ¼ tsp. salt
- 1 egg
- 1 cup milk (230 ml)
- 2 tbsp. cooking oil
- extra cooking oil
- butter and syrup

DIRECTIONS:

1. Measure the dry ingredients (flour, sugar, baking soda, and salt) and mix together in the large measuring cup (or bowl). Set aside.

Facts about pancakes:
1. Pancakes probably came originally from China and Nepal. They came to Europe in the twelfth century with Crusaders, who were returning from the Middle East.
2. Many cultures around the world make some type of pancake. The Russian pancake is the blini, made with yeast and spread with sour cream or caviar.
3. The Chinese make scallion pancakes with rolled dough shaped like a snail.

2. Crack the egg into the large mixing bowl and beat. Add milk and and oil and mix together.

3. Add the dry ingredients and stir well or whisk until batter is lump-free—not too long. If the batter is too thick or thin, add more milk or flour. The thickness of the batter is up to you: thicker means fluffier pancakes, thinner means crisper pancakes.

4. Heat the griddle or skillet to medium-high heat and pour a small amount of oil (start with the size of the bottom of a coffee mug and add more if needed) and spread it over the entire cooking surface with the spatula.

5. Test the heat by getting a drop of water on your fingers and flicking it onto the cook surface. When the water *dances*, it is ready to cook. If it just sits there, continue heating. But, use only

4. *In India thin pancakes called* chapattis *are cooked on a griddle and used to scoop up curries.*

5. *In Britain, on Shrove Tuesday—the end of Lent—people eat pancakes made with sugar and lemon juice.*

6. *At Chanukah, Jews make potato pancakes called* latkes, *which are fried in oil and covered with sour cream or applesauce.*

a drop or two so you don't get splashed and burned.

6. Pour or scoop the batter onto the heated cook surface. The amount you use dictates your pancake size.

7. Flip each pancake when the bubbles that come to the uncooked surface pop and remain open.

8. Cook second side until golden.

9. Serve with butter and syrup.

VARIATIONS:

1. For heartier pancakes: Substitute half (or more) of the flour for whole-wheat flour. These pancakes are not only filled with wonderful wheat, they have a more interesting texture. Note: whole wheat pancakes are likely to use more milk. Since the batter is thicker, bubbles won't necessarily come up through the surface when cooking. So, check for doneness by flipping up an edge with a spatula and look to see if it is browned.

2. For fruitier pancakes: Add blueberries when the batter is finished by folding them in—using your utensil (spoon, whisk, or plastic spatula) to gently scoop under the batter, then pulling it up over the top. You do this because you want to break open as few of the berries as possible. Repeat this until the blueberries are mixed in. These pancakes will take a little longer to cook because the batter next to the moist blueberries will stay uncooked longer—but your patience will be rewarded. Try serving with a fruit syrup. Or, mix a banana and a little milk with a fork and add it into the batter. This batter may also need a little extra milk.

3. Go completely crazy: Add chocolate chips (not too many) into the batter before cooking. Serve with strawberries and whipped cream. 🍎

LUNCHES

LITTLE RED RIDING HOOD
Little Red Riding Hood's Picnic Basket of Goodies:
Deviled Eggs

Granny's Potato Salad

Chicken Salad Pockets

THE MAGIC CAVE
Goat Cheese Sandwiches

THE FOX AND THE GRAPES
Fruit Salad

THE STOLEN BREAD SMELLS
Sweet-Smelling Cinnamon Bread

LITTLE RED RIDING HOOD

Once upon a time there was a little girl who was loved by everyone who knew her, but the one who loved her best was her grandmother. In fact her Granny made the little girl a riding hood of red velvet and after that the child was never seen without it.

Now one day Red Riding Hood's mother said, "I have packed some sandwiches and other goodies in a picnic basket for you to take to Granny. She has been sick and they will do her good. Now, mind you, don't dawdle in the woods."

"I'll go right along," Red Riding Hood answered, and she meant it at the time. But once she got into the woods, it was such a lovely day she decided to pick some flowers to go with the basket of goodies. While she was dawdling, along came a handsome wolf.

Not knowing what a wicked creature he was, Red Riding Hood had no more fear of him than if he had been a large dog. And as this was once upon a time, the wolf could talk.

"Where are you going, Little Red Riding Hood?" asked he.

"To my Granny's" she answered.

"And what's in your picnic basket?" he asked.

"Sandwiches and other goodies," she said. "To give her strength."

"I'm sure it will," said the wolf. "And where does Granny live?"

Suspecting nothing, she told him. He bid her good day and showed her where some exceedingly beautiful trillium grew, down by the brook, then off he went. So Little Red Riding Hood picked flowers until she had a great bouquet of them. Then she got back on the path and headed toward Granny's.

But the wolf had been there before her. He had knocked on the door and when Granny asked, "Who is there?" he had imitated her granddaughter's voice. "Little Red Riding Hood."

"Lift the latch," Granny called out in a tiny voice, "for I am too weak to rise."

The wolf lifted the latch, went inside, leaped onto the bed, and swallowed the old lady whole. Then he put on her extra cap and gown and lay down on the bed, drawing up the quilt to cover himself completely.

Not five minutes later in came Little Red Riding Hood. "Good morning, Granny," she called. "I have a bunch of flowers and a picnic basket quite full of sandwiches and other goodies."

"Set them on the floor," said the wolf, trying to disguise his voice.

"Grandmother, what a rough voice you have," said Little Red Riding Hood.

"That's my cold speaking," whispered the wolf.

The girl came toward the bed and saw the hairy creature in her grandmother's cap. "Why, grandmother, what big ears you have."

"The better to hear you with, my dear."

She came closer. "Why, grandmother, what big eyes you have."

"The better to see you with my dear."

She stood at the side of the bed. "Why, grandmother, what big teeth you have."

"The better to eat you with, my dear!" And saying this, the wolf threw aside the covers and leaped out of bed.

Screaming, Little Red Riding Hood ran toward the door and that very moment, the door was flung open. In stepped a hunter who that very morning had been tracking the wolf.

The most familiar version of this story comes from the Brothers Grimm where it is called "Little Red Cap." However, the earliest published version is in Perrault's 1697 Histories or Tales of Times Past.

The famous writer Charles Dickens wrote that Red Riding Hood had been his first love. "I felt that if I could have married Little Red Riding Hood, I should have known perfect bliss." He would have read the English version that first appeared in 1729.

"Why, you old sinner, I have you now," he cried, aiming his gun and shooting the wolf dead. And when he went to fillet the wolf, who should he find but Granny, still very much alive, though his knife had cut away her white curls.

So Red Riding Hood learned not to stray off the path, the grandmother learned to keep her door bolted, and the hunter—well, he learned to fillet wolves very, very carefully. ⭐

Little Red Riding Hood's Picnic Basket of Goodies

Good enough for Granny or a party of hungry wolves.

Deviled Eggs
(Makes 12 yummy eggs)

 EQUIPMENT:

- pan

- slotted spoon or colander

- bowl and spoon or food processor

- spoon or icing bag with a large star tip

 INGREDIENTS:

- 6 eggs

- ¼ cup mayonnaise (60 ml)

- ½ tsp. dried mustard
- salt and pepper to taste

- paprika

DIRECTIONS:

1. Place the eggs carefully in the pan, cover with cold water and bring to a boil over high heat. Lower the heat to medium-high and boil for 12 minutes.

2. Remove from water with a slotted spoon or by pouring gently into a colander, and let cool.

3. Peel eggs and cut each one in half lengthwise.

4. Gently scoop out the yolks and put them, the mayonnaise, salt, pepper, and dried mustard in the bowl or food processor. Blend until creamy. Add more mayonnaise if necessary. Hint: Always start with less mayonnaise than you need because you can always add more, but you cannot take any out.

5. Scoop the yolk mixture back into the eggs with a spoon or pipe it in through the pastry bag.

6. Top with a small sprinkle of paprika.

VARIATIONS:

Try topping with a slice of green olive or a sprig of fresh parsley instead of paprika.

Act of 1871—was passed because it gave working people time off from their jobs.
4. A picnic basket is also called a picnic hamper.
5. Picnic baskets can come equipped with fine china, silverware, and linen napkins. You have to make the food yourself.
6. Now picnics are big business, and along with the many varieties of picnic baskets, you can also buy picnic tables, picnic backpacks, and insulated coolers. Or you can just carry everything in a paper bag and bring along your fingers and a hearty appetite.

Granny's Potato Salad

Makes enough for a howling good party.

 ### Equipment:

- sharp knife
- cutting board
- peeler
- large pot
- measuring cup
- measuring spoons
- large bowl

 ### Ingredients:

- 6 medium-sized potatoes
- ½ cup mayonnaise (120 ml)
- ¼ cup vegetable oil (60 ml)
- ¼ cup vinegar (60 ml)
- 1 tbsp. parsley, chopped
- ½ onion, chopped small
- 4–6 stalks celery, chopped small
- salt and pepper to taste
- 1 tsp. dill seeds

Directions:

1. Wash the potatoes and boil them in their skins for 20 to 30 minutes or until fork-tender all the way through. (Hint: You can boil the potatoes in the morning or the night before and cool them in the refrigerator.)

2. Drain the potatoes and let them cool.

3. Peel the potatoes with a knife or peeler and chop them into bite-sized pieces.

4. Mix together the mayonnaise, oil, vinegar, parsley, salt, and pepper in the large bowl. This mixture should be a little thicker than heavy cream.

5. Add the chopped onions, celery, and dill seeds and mix.

6. Add the potatoes and mix.

7. Cover and refrigerate until time to serve. If salad is dry, mix a bit more sauce (step 4) and add it in.

VARIATIONS:

Remember, the type of mayonnaise you chose will drastically change the taste of your potato salad. Experiment with different kinds to see which one you like the best.

To change this recipe you can delete items such as the onions if you are not a big fan of them, or try red potatoes instead of regular. Try additional ingredients to make the potato salad even more interesting: chop up the whites of 4 hard-boiled eggs and add them; try diced green, yellow, and/or red peppers; or toss in some fresh or frozen peas. ●

Chicken Salad Pockets

The better to eat, my dear. (Makes 6–7 servings)

For this recipe you can use leftover chicken instead of preparing an entire chicken. Just remember: if you are using a smaller amount of leftover chicken, lessen the amounts of the other ingredients too.

EQUIPMENT:

- large stockpot
- large serving fork or tongs
- large bowl
- knife
- cutting board
- peeler
- large spoon
- measuring cup

INGREDIENTS:

- 1 whole chicken
- ½ cup mayonnaise (120 ml)
- 1 large celery stalk, chopped
- 1 green apple, cubed and tossed with a sprinkle of lemon juice
- 1 tsp. lemon juice plus more for sprinkling on the apple
- 1 tsp. balsamic vinegar
- ¼ cup chopped walnuts (40 g)
- salt and pepper to taste
- pocket bread
- Brie cheese (optional)

DIRECTIONS:

1. Remove the giblets (liver and other parts in a plastic bag) from inside the chicken and throw out (or set aside if someone will use them later.) Rinse the chicken in cool water and place it in a large stock pot. Fill with water to cover the chicken, sprinkle in some salt and pepper, and bring to a boil over high heat. Lower to medium heat and cook for an hour. Remove chicken carefully with a large serving fork, tongs, or both, and set aside to cool. When cool, remove all the meat from the bones with your fingers and a knife. Chop the meat into small pieces. This makes about 4 cups and can be replaced with leftover chicken. The chicken stock left in the pot can be saved for another recipe or frozen.

2. Mix chicken and mayonnaise in large bowl.

3. Wash and chop celery and peel, chop, and toss the apple with lemon juice so it does not turn brown.

4. Add the apple, celery, salt, pepper, lemon juice, vinegar, and walnuts to the chicken mixture and toss together.

5. Cut the top inch from each pocket bread.

6. Spread the Brie on the inside of each pocket with a butter knife.

7. Fill with chicken salad and serve.

THE MAGIC CAVE

Once near a small Polish village there lived a poor Jewish farmer named Shimon and his wife, Gert. Though they had no money, they never cursed their fate. Rather they would go to the synagogue every Sabbath and pray.

"For though we have little," the Shimon said to his wife, "we have more than many."

And indeed they did. They had two goats that gave them milk— a little but enough—and with the goat's milk they made butter and cheese for themselves and some to sell at market.

A little—but enough.

Now one evening, when Gert went to bring in the goats from the field, they were not there. Gone. Vanished.

Shimon and Gert searched high, they searched low, they searched all the fields around, but the goats were nowhere to be found.

Then Gert began to weep into her apron but Shimon said, "Everything is from Heaven. We do not yet know what this means."

This story is still told in Poland and in Israel. It is similar to many stories about underground passages leading to the Holy Land.

Some of the versions are told as folktales though one popular version was written down by the great Yiddish writer Sh. Y. Agnon.

"Means?" cried Gert, "it means we will go hungry." But she stopped her wailing long enough to go into the house and to light the evening's candles.

Just then Shimon ran in shouting, "They have come home. And see! See!"

Gert ran outside and sure enough, there were the goats, their udders swollen with milk. And when Gert milked them, there was twice as much milk as ever before. "Oh my husband, how right you are. Everything indeed, is from Heaven!"

• • •

Well, the next evening it was the same. The goats vanished from the fields and could not be found. But after the candles were lit, they suddenly appeared at the barn door, their udders swollen with milk, more milk than ever.

"A miracle!" said Shimon, and Gert agreed.

And even more miraculous, the milk seemed to heal the sick, and the cheese to cure the dying. Soon no one in the little village had so much as a hangnail.

• • •

Six days passed, miracle after miracle. But on the seventh day, Shimon said to Gert, "I must follow the goats and see where they go. For what if this miracle is of the devil's making?"

"Good healing milk could never be from the Evil One," said Gert, spitting through her fingers to ward off the wicked one.

"But husband, if you are determined to go, I will go with you. Nothing should separate a man and his wife."

So they followed the goats around the field and through a forest that was wide in some places and narrow in others. They climbed after them when the goats went up the mountain. And at last, they followed the goats into a dark cave.

"Hold onto my coattails," Shimon said as they entered the cave. "Do not be afraid." He did not say that he was a little afraid himself. "Heaven will protect us."

They had gone but a little way into the cave when they saw afar a bright, shining light. The goats scrambled ahead toward the light and Shimon and Gert followed after.

Suddenly devils and imps leaped out at them. Stones rained down from the cave walls.

"Do not be afraid," whispered Gert in Shimon's ear. "Heaven will protect us."

A number of the parts of this story can be found as traveling motifs in other stories, including: Underground Passage Magically Opens, D1555; Journey to an Earthly Paradise, 111; Treasure-Producing Goat, B103.0.5.

This reminder heartened Shimon and so the two went ahead, looking neither left nor right. When the devils and imps saw they could make no impression on the two—nor separate them—they disappeared back to the dark regions of dreams.

Shimon and Gert followed the goats all the way to the light, and then through it. When they came out the other side of the cave, they found themselves standing in a green and fertile valley.

Nearby was a young shepherd, playing on his pipe.

"Who are you?" asked Shimon.

"And where are we?" asked Gert.

The shepherd boy took the pipe from his mouth. "My name is Dov," he said. And "down there," he thrust out his hand, "is the holy city of Jerusalem."

How strange! From Poland to Jerusalem is a long and arduous trip. It takes many months of walking. Yet here they were!

"A miracle indeed," said Shimon to Gert. "Let us tell all our cousins to follow the goats here to the Holy Land."

So they wrote a letter to the people of the town, wrapped the letter in a fig leaf, and tied the fig leaf to one of the goats.

That night the goats went back through the cave to Poland. They were found the next day by a man who lived in the village, but he did not notice the fig leaf. Instead he knocked on the door of the house but old Shimon and Gert were gone.

For six days the villager came to check on them, but they never came back. Fearing the worst, he took the goats to his house, but as they could not be cared for in town, they were taken to the slaughterhouse where they were killed for their meat. Only then was the note found—too late. The goats could no longer show the people of the town how to find the cave.

So the rabbi kept the letter in the synagogue, and when he died, it was in the keeping of the next rabbi. And finally, when the little town was burned down in the Great Holocaust, the letter was gone as well.

And all that is left is this story. ⭐

Goat Cheese Sandwiches

So delicious, you'll think you're in heaven. (Serves 2–3)

EQUIPMENT:

- cutting board
- sharp knife
- peeler (optional)
- clean scissors (optional)
- measuring spoons
- small bowl
- whisk or fork
- spoon
- butter knife

INGREDIENTS:

- 1 12-inch (30 cm) baguette or other unsliced bread
- 3 small tomatoes or 1 large tomato
- 1 cucumber (medium-sized or half a larger one)
- 6 fresh basil leaves
- 1 tbsp. balsamic vinegar
- 1 tbsp. extra virgin olive oil
- dash of salt
- dash of pepper
- 4 oz. mild goat cheese (120 g)
- slices of purple onion (optional)

Facts about goat cheese:

1. Goat cheese and olive oil are amoung the first manufactured foods still being eaten today.

2. Most goat cheese is made on small farms.

3. Goat cheese is also called by its French name, chevre. *It is very important in the French diet.*

DIRECTIONS:

1. Slice the tomatoes. Peel and slice the cucumber. Cut the basil leaves into strips with scissors or a knife and set them all aside.

2. Cut the bread lengthwise and set out with both cut sides up.

3. Measure and mix together the olive oil and balsamic vinegar with the salt and pepper in the small bowl using a fork or whisk.

4. Spoon the oil and vinegar mixture onto both cut sides of the bread. Because the vinegar is dark, you can see if it is evenly distributed.

5. Spread the goat cheese onto the bottom half of the bread.

6. Layer the tomatoes, then the cucumbers, and finally the basil atop the goat cheese. Add slices of onion if you want.

7. Put the top bread on the sandwich and press down lightly.

Either wrap the sandwich tightly in plastic wrap and refrigerate it or cut the sandwich into as many slices as you want. The slices can be held together with toothpicks. 🍅

4. Unlike cow cheeses, goat cheeses are usually not left to age, which is why they look so fresh and creamy.

5. Other ways to eat goat cheese: in a salad, on toasted bagels, in lasagna, in place of sour cream on baked potatoes, in cheesecake.

6. Besides cows and goats, other milk-producing animals used in cheese-making are sheep, buffalo, and zebu.

THE FOX AND THE GRAPES

On a hot summer's day, the sun broiling the countryside, a fox strolled through an orchard. He had nothing in mind, just ambling along.

All at once he came to a bunch of grapes that were ripening on a trellised vine.

He sniffed, suddenly both hungry and thirsty. "Just the thing for a hot summer's day."

Drawing back a few paces, the fox then ran forward and leaped into the air, snapping at the grapes with his teeth. But he missed

This fable is one of many credited to the great Greek storyteller Aesop. Little is known about him. According to some sources, he was a deformed slave who lived on the island of Samos in the sixth century BCE. It is said he was freed by his master as a reward for his great learning. As a free man, he became an ambassador for King Croesus of Lydia (now part of Turkey) who ruled from 560 to 546 BCE. Eventually, Aesop was executed in Delphi while on a mission for the king.

by no more than an inch and his teeth clicked together: snip-snip-snap!

Turning around, he went a little further back, then ran forward faster, jumped higher, but-alas–missed again.

A third, a fourth, and a fifth time he tried to get that tempting morsel, but each jump was less successful than the last.

Finally, panting and perspiring under the hot sun, he walked away with his nose in the air. "I didn't want those grapes anyway," he told himself. "I'm quite sure they're sour." ⭐

Did Aesop really write all the fables credited to him? Some scholars believe that these tales were collected from many different sources and were not all written by one man. Some scholars even believe the fables were written by a woman.

Aesop's fables have had a number of retellers, including Babrius, Phaedrus, and most notably the French writer La Fontaine who put them down in verse. In modern times the stories have often been made into children's books as single stories as well as collections of the most popular tales.

Fruit Salad

Use only sweet fruit—never sour. (Serves a family or a party)

EQUIPMENT:

- sharp knife
- melon-baller (optional)
- cutting board
- rubber spatula

INGREDIENTS:

- Fruit—any kind!

Good options include: watermelon, cantaloupe, honeydew melon, pineapple, strawberries, star fruit, apples, oranges, tangerines, peaches—and of course grapes.

For the top (fruit you don't want to mix in because they are more delicate—and pretty), try one or several of these: blueberries, blackberries, raspberries, or kiwi.

DIRECTIONS:

1. Wash and prepare the fruit:

Melon: cut in half, discard the seeds, and scoop out the flesh with a melon-baller or a spoon. Melons can also be cut into cubes with a knife.

Citrus, such as oranges: peel and remove pith (white part). Section, remove seeds and cut into chunks.

Other fruits: Peel, if necessary, and cut into chunks.

2. Squeeze an orange and pour the juice over the fruit salad.

3. Mix with the rubber spatula.

4. Put topping fruit(s) on top, cover and refrigerate until ready to eat.

VARIATIONS:

All fruit salads are different depending on the seasonal fruit available. Some fruit can be pre-cut (and even canned), but always use as much fresh fruit as possible. Putting your fruit salad in a carved out watermelon is always a welcome party treat. 🍎

4. Many insects can damage grapes: grape leafroller, climbing cutworm, flea beetles, grape berry moth, aphids, and Japanese beetles among others.

5. In the United States, 97 percent of table grapes are grown in California.

6. Grapes can be used in many ways: eaten plain; dried for raisins; made into juice, wine, jelly, and jams; or as sweeteners in other cooked products.

THE STOLEN BREAD SMELLS

Once in a small town in the middle of the country there was a baker known far and wide as Mr. Stingy because he never gave away free samples. But as he was the finest baker around, the local people still bought bread at his shop.

Now, day after day when Mr. Stingy made his bread, the smell floated from the ovens, through the keyhole of the closed front door, and out into the street. It was that smell—delicious and enticing—that always brought buyers into his shop.

Mr. Stingy liked the fact that the smell brought people in. But one day he noticed that there was one man, with a raggedy coat and no hat, who stood outside and simply sniffed and sniffed the bread smell but did not come in to buy.

"Look at him," Mr. Stingy whispered. "Stealing my bread smells! Filling himself up—and nothing in it for me." He waved his fist at the beggar, but the man did not move.

"Get away! Get away!" shouted Mr. Stingy at the beggar. But still the man did not move. He just sniffed and sniffed some more.

At last the stingy baker could stand it no longer. He called 911 and when the police arrived, he had them arrest the beggar.

"He's a thief!" Mr. Stingy cried.

The beggar was hauled off to jail and that afternoon (this is a fairy tale after all) he was brought before a judge. The charge: theft of bread smell.

Quickly the judge made his decision. (Definitely a fairy tale!) He said to the beggar, "Have you any coins?"

The beggar reached into his worn pants pocket and pulled out a worn copper penny and one thin dime. "That's it, m'Lord."

He handed the two coins to the judge.

The judge rattled the coins and they clinked together. He turned to the baker. "Hear that?"

Confused, the baker nodded.

"That's your payment. The sound of coins as payment for the theft of smells." ⭐

In Cambodia the story concerns an old man resting in the shade thrown by an ox. He, too, pays with a shadow of a coin.

Often the judgment in the story is handed down by a well-known folk character. In the Middle Eastern version, the wise-fool Hodja solves the problem. In the Burmese story, it is the clever and fair Princess Learned-in-the-Law who figures out the best solution.

Sweet-Smelling Cinnamon Bread

Smells so good your family might just sneak a whiff. (Makes 1 or 2 loaves)

EQUIPMENT:

- measuring cup
- food processor with steel blade
- measuring spoons
- pan
- rolling pin
- large bowl
- wet cloth
- loaf pan(s)

INGREDIENTS:

- 3 cups all-purpose flour (400 g)
- 1 tsp. salt
- 1¼ cups lukewarm water (290 ml)
- 1 tbsp. butter
- 1 tbsp. sugar
- 1 packet active dry yeast
- 1 tbsp. vegetable oil
- extra flour
- 2 tbsp. sugar
- 1 tsp. cinnamon

DIRECTIONS:

1. Measure the flour and salt and pour into the food processor. (You can do without the processor—it'll just take more time and muscle.)

2. Melt the butter at low heat and add the water, sugar and yeast. Let sit for 5 minutes.

3. Close the food processor and turn on. Pour the water mixture through the feeding tube (the hole in the top). Let the food processor continue running until the dough is completely mixed.

4. Sprinkle some flour onto a clean work surface and on your hands and remove the dough from the food processor (carefully because the blade is sharp).

5. Knead the dough for 2 minutes, adding more flour to your hands if it is too sticky. Make the dough into a ball.

6. Coat the large bowl with the vegetable oil and place the ball of dough into it, turning once to coat with oil. Cover with a wet (but not dripping) cloth and put the bowl in a warm place so the dough can rise for one hour.

7. Preheat oven to 350 degrees.

8. Decide whether you want to make one large loaf or two smaller loaves. If you choose two, separate the dough into two pieces now.

4. English bakers of white and brown breads originally had separate guilds. Queen Elizabeth I united them into The Worshipful Company of Bakers.
5. Besides the flat-breads eaten around the world (pita, chap-ati, tortillas, etc.) there are two basic breads—leavened or raised bread made with yeast, and quick breads made with baking powder.
6. Quick breads were developed in 18th-century America using an ingredient called pearlash, made from wood ash. In 1857 baking powder was first made commercially.

9. Knead the dough and roll it out with the rolling pin until flat.

10. Mix the cinnamon and sugar together in a small bowl and sprinkle the mixture onto the dough.

11. Roll the dough up from each side toward the middle, tucking the unrolled ends in before you are done. Pinch the top to hold the dough together.

12. Butter the loaf pan(s) and put in the rolled dough.

13. Cook for 40 minutes for two small loaves or 50 minutes for one large loaf.

14. Serve with butter.

VARIATIONS:

You can cook this bread without adding the cinnamon sugar, just as plain bread. Or try rolling it into balls or twisting it into sticks and coating it with the cinnamon sugar.

Soups

Brer Rabbit
Carrot Soup

Share Crops
Corn Chowder

Stone Soup
Stone Soup

BRER RABBIT

In the not so long ago, Brer Rabbit was cutting capers all over the place and acting like he was King of the World.

Well, Brer Fox, who'd been fooled once or a dozen times by Brer Rabbit, thought it was time to teach the pesky critter a lesson. And a sticky lesson it promised to be.

Brer Fox found some tar and he mixed it with turpentine. Then he patted it and molded it into a critter he called Tar Baby. He placed a straw hat on top of Tar Baby's head and put a corncob pipe in its mouth and set it right down in the middle of the road. Then he lay down in the bushes to watch what would happen as Tar Baby got thick and sticky in the sun.

He didn't have long to wait because who should come down the road—lippity-lappity, clippity-clappity—but Brer Rabbit. He was singing and dancing and having a good old time.

But Brer Fox he just lay low.

Then Brer Rabbit saw Tar Baby in the middle of the road.

"Good morning," said Brer Rabbit. "Nice weather. Good for

This story first appeared in print in Joel Chandler Harris's 1883 book of Uncle Remus stories. Written in heavy dialect, the stories are put in the mouth of a slave character on an old Southern plantation. As a boy Harris (who was white) had worked on such a plantation and he claimed he had heard the stories that slaves told for entertainment and simply wrote them down. According to Stith Thompson, the Tar Baby story (type 175) began in the Indian Jataka tales, then migrated to Africa, finally coming to America with the slaves.

growing things like carrots and taters. I just love carrots and taters. How about you?"

Well, Tar Baby didn't say a word. And Brer Fox, he just lay low.

"You feeling all right?" asked Brer Rabbit coming closer. "Can I help?"

Of course Tar Baby didn't say a word. And Brer Fox, he just lay low.

"Well, then, aren't you a stuck-up, can't be bothered, touch-me-never," said Brer Rabbit, hoping to get a rise out of Tar Baby.

But Tar Baby never said a word. And Brer Fox, he just lay low.

"Speak to me, now!" yelled Brer Rabbit. "Or I swear I'm gonna have to teach you a lesson." He drew back a fist.

But Tar Baby never said a word. And Brer Fox, he just lay low.

So Brer Rabbit he wound up and socked that Tar Baby right in the jaw. But his fist went deep into the tar, and pull as he might, Brer Rabbit couldn't haul it out again.

Still Tar Baby never said a word. And Brer Fox, he just lay low.

"Let me loose, you consarned silent impling, or I'll hit you with my other fist," cried Brer Rabbit.

But Tar Baby never said a word. And Brer Fox, he just lay low.

So Brer Rabbit up and walloped Tar Baby with his other fist and the same thing happened. The fist sunk into the tar and was held fast.

"Let me go, or I'll kick your lights out," yelled Brer Rabbit. "And I can do it, too, with my big back feet."

But Tar Baby never said a word. And Brer Fox, he just lay low.

So Brer Rabbit kicked Tar Baby with his right leg and he kicked Tar Baby with his left leg, and they both sunk into the tar, and now Brer Rabbit he was stuck fast.

Just then Brer Fox strolled out from behind the bushes. He looked Brer Rabbit up and looked him down. Then he smiled a long, slow, sly smile. "Howdy, Brer Rabbit. It ain't the Tar Baby's whose stuck up—it's you!" He laughed. "And now I'm gonna slow roast you for sure."

Well, Brer Rabbit knew he was in trouble, because trouble was his business after all. So he said, "I don't care what you do with me, Brer Fox. Roast me or toast me or make me into shish-kebab, but just don't fling me into that briar patch yonder."

Brer Fox looked over at the briar patch with its sharp thorns. Then he said, "Too much trouble building a fire. I 'spect I'll just drown you."

"I don't care what you do to me, Brer Fox," said Brer Rabbit. "Water up the nose and down the toes, and water dripping off my powder-puff tail, so long as you don't fling me into that briar patch yonder."

There is a fine Native American version, quite possibly brought into the tradition by a runaway slave—or even a freeman of color who married into the tribe—about a gum baby.

And though today Harris's dialect seems demeaning, African-American authors and readers have nevertheless embraced the trickster rabbit—so like the tortoise, spider, and hare of African tales—as their own. Who wouldn't? Brer Rabbit always has the last laugh.

Brer Fox looked again at the briar patch with its needle-sharp thorns. "Not a lot of water close by," he said, "and I don't want to be hauling you over here and half of Texas. I 'spect I'll just hang you."

"I don't care what you do to me, Brer Fox," said Brer Rabbit. "Hang me high or hang me low, or hang me upside-over, so long as you don't fling me into that briar patch yonder."

Brer Fox looked again at the briar patch with its extra sharp thorns. "Got no rope," he said. "Got nowhere to find one. But I got the best idea of all." He grabbed up Brer Rabbit round the middle and plucked him out of the tar with a sound like a great big slurp. Then he swung Brer Rabbit three times around and flung him into the middle of that thorny patch. "Lie there in that prickery bed!" he shouted, "cause it's the one place you don't want to be!"

Well, Brer Rabbit landed in the middle of the patch and started laughing and a-singing out, "Born and bred in the briar patch, Brer Fox! Born and bred in the briar patch!"

Then Brer Fox he lay down in the middle of the road and beat his head in the dirt. He howled and howled and howled some more because once again he'd been fooled by Brer Rabbit. ⭐

Carrot Soup

Eat it while you lay low. (Makes 8 servings)

EQUIPMENT:

- sharp knife
- cutting board
- peeler
- large pot
- measuring cup
- large spoon or spatula
- zesting tool or cheese grater
- blender
- large bowl

INGREDIENTS:

- 2 tbsp. butter
- 1 pound carrots (large or baby), peeled and chopped (450 g)
- 2 potatoes, peeled and chopped
- 1 onion, chopped
- 1 clove of garlic
- 3 cups water (1.5 pints or 700 ml)
- 1 tsp. vegetable bouillon (5 ml)
- fresh basil (about 6 leaves)
- juice from half an orange or ¼ cup (60 ml) orange juice
- ½ tsp. orange zest
- salt and pepper
- heavy cream

DIRECTIONS:

1. Prepare the carrots and potatoes by washing them, peeling them (though baby carrots don't need to be peeled), and cutting them all into small pieces. Peel and chop the onion. Peel the papery outer layer from the garlic and trim the ends. Mix the water and vegetable bouillon together in the measuring cup. Set aside.

2. Melt the butter in the large pot at medium heat.

3. Add the carrots, potatoes, onion, and garlic and mix with the spoon or spatula until the melted butter coats them all.

4. Add the bouillon/water mixture and the basil and bring to a boil at high heat.

5. Lower the temperature to medium and boil for 7 minutes or until carrots are soft.

6. Zest the orange: using a zesting tool or a cheese grater, peel small pieces of the skin from a clean orange. Scrape only the sweet orange skin and not the pith (the bitter white between the skin and the fruit).

7. Cut the orange in half and squeeze the juice from one half into the measuring cup or a new bowl.

8. Add the orange zest and juice, and salt and pepper to taste to the pot and cook for one more minute.

5. Carrots come in many shades—red, purple, yellow, black, white. However, the orange carrot is the most common. These were developed by the Dutch in the Middle Ages.
6. Although it is poisonous, Queen Anne's lace is a kind of wild carrot. It is also called birds' nest weed, bees' nest, and rantipole.

93

9. Turn off the heat and scoop portions of the mixture into a blender and blend until fairly smooth (small chunks only make the soup better). Pour out into the large bowl and scoop more into the blender. Repeat until all the soup is pureed and in the bowl.

10. Serve with a dollop (about a tablespoon) of cream and a sprinkling of fresh basil.

VARIATIONS:

Instead of the onion and garlic, use two sweet apples peeled, cored, and cut into small pieces.

Or instead of basil, use fresh parsley. Experiment with other herbs—a good test is to smell them and ask yourself if they smell as if they should go in your dish. 🍅

SHARE CROPS

High John had been a slave, but he was a slave no longer. He went to his old master and said, "Boss, I'm a good farmer but I got no land. Will you let me rent from you?"

And Boss said, "We'll share. You do the work and we'll go halves."

"What kind of halves, Boss?" asked High John.

Boss smiled. "I get the tops, you get the bottoms, John." And that was that.

So that summer John planted potatoes.

And when it came time to harvest, Boss was not pleased. He stomped his foot because he got the green tops, but High John got the taters.

"Now, John, you fooled me once, you won't fool me again. Next year I get the bottoms, you get the tops." And that was that.

Well, the next summer John planted squash and when Boss came along for the harvest, he got only the roots while High John got the gourds.

Boss was really not pleased this time. He stomped his foot and shook his fist. "John, you fooled me twice, but you won't fool me again. Next year I get both bottoms and tops and you get what's in-between." And that was that.

Well, that next summer High John planted corn, and when Boss came along for the harvest, he got the roots and the tassels but John got the ears.

Boss was not pleased. Not pleased at all. He stomped his foot and shook his fist and said all kinds of swears. But he had learned his lesson.

That's when High John said, "Next year, Boss, if we go half and half, share and share alike, you'll be pleased."

And he was. ⭐

This story is so popular, it has its own tale type: 1030, Crop Division. And its own motif number: K171.1, Deceptive crop division, above the ground, below the ground.

Of course, depending on where the tale is told, the crops differ as well. Carrots or turnips might take the place of the potatoes in this story, and so forth—just as a cook might make some substitutions in a stew.

Corn Chowder

To share and share alike. (Serves a family)

EQUIPMENT:

- cutting board
- peeler
- sharp knife
- garlic press (optional)
- measuring cup
- sauce pan (medium to large)
- small bowl

INGREDIENTS:

- 1 medium potato, peeled, and chopped into small cubes
- ½ medium onion, chopped fine
- 1 clove garlic, pressed
- 3 tbsp. butter
- 1 chicken bouillon cube dissolved in 1 cup (230 ml) water (or 1 cup chicken stock)
- 2 cups of fresh, frozen, or canned corn
- 1 cup milk (230 ml)
- 1 cup cream (230 ml)
- ½ tsp. salt
- ¼ tsp. pepper
- mixture of ¼ cup (60 ml) milk and 2 tbsp. flour

DIRECTIONS:

1. Peel the potato and chop it and the onion. Peel and press or mince the garlic. Set aside.

2. Melt the butter in the pan at medium heat.

3. Add onions, potatoes, garlic, and corn to the pan and coat with butter. Add the water and bouillon (or stock).

4. Bring to a boil at high heat then lower heat to medium. Cook, stirring frequently, at a light boil for 25 minutes or until the potatoes are soft when poked with a fork.

5. Add the milk and cream slowly to pan of vegetables.

6. Stir in the flour/milk mixture slowly.

7. Stir and cook for 5 minutes more.

8. Add salt and pepper and serve.

VARIATIONS:

For a heartier chowder, try adding cooked chicken or bacon to the chowder after step 6. 🍅

4. *Corn is in the grass family* Tripsaceae, *Its seeds are cereal grains, its ear part of the flower.*

5. *Corn is the second most plentiful grain in the world after rice. Corn as we know it today is the only food plant that cannot reproduce without the help of man.*

6. *The most common kinds of corn are flint (Indian corn), dent (field corn for livestock and industrial products), flour (for tortillas, chips, baked goods), sweet (for eating), and popcorn.*

STONE SOUP

In old Portugal there lived a monk, a quiet monk, a man of faith and poverty, who wandered through the country villages in his brown monk's robe and cowl in search of his daily meal. He did this because of a promise he had made, a promise to God, which is not the kind of promise to break. Especially if one is a monk.

One day he came to the village of Desperanza, as desperate as its name. He knocked on one door after another, but no one had so much as a crust of bread for him. Indeed, they shouted at him and cursed him and shut their doors in his face.

Now the monk knew that he must go hungry, but hunger was nothing new for him. Worse, if he left because of the villagers' shouts and curses, he would leave them to their ignorance and anger, to their unkindness and greed.

So at the last house, when he knocked on the door, he asked the woman of the house–before she could curse him–if he might borrow a pot for an hour or so.

She was so astonished, she said yes. And more astonished still when he took a stone from under his brown robe and placed it in the pot.

"What are you doing, father?" she asked.

"I am making *sopa de pedra*, stone soup," he replied.

"No one can make soup from a stone," the woman said.

"With the right stone it is easy," said the monk. "Easy, and cheap, and delicious."

Well, the woman had to watch as the monk went to her well and got water for the stone soup. "Easy and cheap and delicious," she whispered, though she lingered on the word *cheap*. "Just the thing!"

The monk put the pot onto the fire and gazed into it. "Of course *sopa de pedra* is always better with a bit of onion."

The woman nodded. "Any soup is better that way." And she went to her cold bin and brought him not one onion but two.

Soon the woman's daughter came to visit and watched the making of stone soup. "Better yet, a bit of celery," she said and raced home for some. Along the way she told others about the monk and his soup from a stone.

No one wanted to be left out: imagine, easy, cheap, and delicious soup made from a stone! (They all lingered on the word *cheap*.) And so this one brought some beans, and that one some beef, and another a turnip and carrot, and another potatoes.

Soon the aroma of the stone soup filled the little house.

Surprise! There was enough soup for the entire village and, when he left to go on his way, the monk gave them the stone as a token of his gratitude. "For this stone will always make a good soup as long as you work on it together," he said.

Do you not believe me? That stone still sits in a velvet-lined box in the village church, where once a year it is used to cook a splendid meal for all. ⭐

In 1947, right after World War II, American children's book author-illustrator Marcia Brown set the story in eighteenth-century France. The book won the Caldecott Medal for the most distin-guished picture book of the year and became an instant childhood classic.

Today the story is not only used in classrooms around the world, but told from pulpits and even assigned as reading for missionary groups. Soup kitchens and cafés have been named Stone Soup, as has a magazine that publishes stories and poems written by children.

Stone Soup

Make it yourself or with your village. (Serves a family)

Facts about soup:

1. The word soup is related to the word *sop,* meaning a piece of bread soaked in liquid, though soup itself clearly goes back to prehistoric times.

2. The world's cultures each have their own special soups. Chinese have egg drop soup. Russians make borscht from beets. The Spanish invented gazpacho, the French pot-au-feu, *the Scots cock-a-leekie soup.*

3. One of the oldest references to soup comes from a Chinese poem of the third century BCE.

EQUIPMENT:

- large stock pot
- measuring cup
- sharp knife
- peeler
- cutting board
- garlic press (optional)

Note: All vegetables and herbs can have substitutes, but try to guess how much cooking time they need and add them to that group.

INGREDIENTS:

- 1 rock (big enough not to be mistaken for food)
- 2 tablespoons butter or oil
- group A vegetables:

1 large clove garlic, minced

1 onion

1 sweet pepper

2 celery stalks

2 carrots

5 or 6 mushrooms

- group B vegetables:

5 small potatoes

2 summer squash or zucchini

- group C vegetables:

1 tomato

1 big handful of green beans

1 handful of parsley

- 6 cups vegetable stock (1.4 liters)
- salt and pepper
- grated romano or parmesan cheese

DIRECTIONS:

1. Scrub and boil the rock, or clean and use one of the small potatoes for rocks. (They do taste better).

2. Wash and chop all the vegetables in groups A, B, and C.

3. Melt the butter in the stock pot.

4. Sauté group A vegetables for 15 minutes or until tender.

5. Add the vegetable stock and rock and bring to a boil

6. Add group B vegetables and lower heat.

7. Boil for 2 minutes.

8. Add group C vegetables and cook for 10 minutes more.

9. Serve with grated cheese.

VARIATIONS: *Throw a stone soup party: Ask each guest to bring his or her favorite vegetable and make the soup together. But remember to have back-ups in case everyone brings carrots.* 🍅

4. On their exploration across North America, Lewis and Clark brought along 193 pounds of "Portable Soup," a dried soup made of beans and vegetables. Just add water and boil!

5. Gangster Al Capone set up Chicago's very first soup kitchen in the 1930s to feed the poor.

DINNERS

THE LITTLE MERMAID
Seaweed Stuffed Shells
Tomato Sauce

HODJA BORROWS A POT
Hodja's Kebabs
Cucumber Yogurt Salad

THE THREE LEMONS
Lemon Chicken
Caesar Salad

THE GREAT TURNIP
Mashed Turnips

JACK AND THE BEANSTALK
Jack's Magic Party Beans

THE LITTLE MERMAID

Down in the deepest part of the ocean is the place where the Sea-folk dwell. And you mustn't think it is only a bare sandbank. Oh, no! Trees and plants grow there, their leaves and stalks waving in the slightest motion of the water. Fishes glide through the branches. And in the very middle of the deepest part of the ocean is the Sea-king's palace. The walls are made of coral and the roof of mussel-shells that open and shut according to the tides.

Now the Sea-king had long been a widower, so his old mother kept house for him. She was a wise woman who was very proud of being a king's mother, and took loving care of her six beautiful granddaughters, though the one she loved best was the youngest.

This little mermaid had skin like a rose petal, eyes as blue as the sea, and like all the other Sea-folk, she had no feet but a long, silvery-green fishtail. She loved to play hide-and-seek with her sisters among the sea trees, and tag around the anemones. But most of all, she loved to hear about the world above, where humans walked on two legs along dry streets. It sounded so odd and so beautiful.

Though this sounds like an old fairy tale, it was written by Danish author, Hans Christian Andersen in the middle of the 19th century. Son of a poor shoemaker and his illiterate wife, Andersen left school at an early age, but being a great reader, he found success. In his thirties, Andersen began writing fairy tales, some of them versions of the stories his mother used to tell, and some wholly new. He published over a hundred such tales, as well as poetry, plays, essays, and novels.

"When you reach your fifteenth year," her grandmother told her, "you will be allowed to Rise and sit upon a rock in the moonlight and see all this for yourself. But never love a land-man, child. Their lives are shorter than ours by hundreds of years. When they die, their souls go up to the stars. But we turn into sea foam."

One by one her older sisters got to Rise and they all came back excited about what they had seen: birds that fluttered overhead calling out songs, flowers that let forth a heavenly perfume, and people walking the land streets on two legs.

"Oh, how I wish I were fifteen," cried the little mermaid each time. "I know I shall love the world above, and all the folk who live there."

• • •

And then one day, she was finally old enough. Her grandmother placed a wreath of white water lilies in her hair and sent her above.

The first thing the little mermaid saw was a great black ship. As she swam closer, she raised herself up to look through the cabin window. Inside, many finely dressed two-legged people danced about. Her eyes were drawn to the handsomest one there, the young prince who was being celebrated for his sixteenth birthday. All around him lamps glowed and music played. When he turned away for a moment and smiled out towards the window, the little mermaid thought he was smiling just for her.

Suddenly, in the midst of all the music and laughter, there came a more ominous sound. A sudden storm blew up and the huge ship pitched to and fro. Water rose up like black mountains and the ship struggled and strained. There was a sudden crack! and the ship heeled over and sank beneath the waves.

The little mermaid cared nothing for the other land folk, but she was desperate to save the smiling prince. She swam through the waters, past the planks and spars of the broken ship, until she found him. Then, holding his head above water, she managed to bring him to the shore. Then she scrambled back into the water where she watched over him until he should wake.

Just then a number of land girls came down to the water's edge and found the prince and carried him away to one of their buildings. And the little mermaid did not see him again.

• • •

The little mermaid swam back to her father's palace, sad and thoughtful. When she told her grandmother what had happened, her grandmother said, "I told you not to love a land-man." But the little mermaid could not help it. She made herself sick with longing.

She left her father's palace and sought out the wicked sea witch who had hideous water snakes curling about her shoulders.

"You are a fool," said the sea witch, "but I shall help you anyway." She gave the little mermaid a potion to turn her lovely

Like the Ugly Duckling, one of his own creations, Andersen was homely and often unloved. But he became one of the most famous Danes who ever lived. His stories have been published in almost every language in the world.

A statue of the Little Mermaid sits in Denmark's capital city Copenhagen, gazing out towards the sea.

In New York City's Central Park is a statue of Andersen, an open book on his lap, in front of which storytellers tell tales.

tail into legs, though she warned, "Walking on them will be like walking on sharp knives." And further the sea witch told her, "My payment will be your lovely voice. But this you must understand— should your prince wed another, you will be turned into foam that very night."

So the little mermaid gave the wicked sea witch her voice, and took the potion. Then she rose out of the sea, near the palace where the prince had been taken. There she drank down the potion. It felt as if a sword had been driven through her body and she was swept by a wave onto the shore.

• • •

When little mermaid woke, the prince was walking down on the seashore and saw her. He asked where she was from but, of course she couldn't say for she no longer had a voice. Then he led her to the palace, and every step she took was so painful, she felt as if knives had been driven into her feet.

Still, everyone was enchanted with her, and she was so happy to be close to the prince and become his companion and sister, the pain did not matter.

And so she remained for many months.

But one day it was announced that on that very eve, the prince would be married to the princess of the castle, the one who with her maidens had found him half-drowned on the shore.

The little mermaid was frightened and went down to the beach where her sisters rose up to see her. She told them with her hands what had happened. They promised to be back that night.

• • •

When they rose from the deep again, the little mermaid was shocked to see they had cut off all their long hair. "We have given it to the sea witch," they said, "in exchange for this knife." It was a knife with which the little mermaid could win her freedom—and the return of her tail—by plunging the dagger into the prince's heart. With a great collective sigh, her sisters dove back into the sea.

The little mermaid took the knife and went back to the palace. She found the room where the prince and his new bride lay sleeping in one another's arms. Drawing aside the curtain of their bed, she stared at them, but she could not bring herself to strike.

Racing down to the seashore, pain knifing through her feet, the little mermaid saw that the sun was setting. Night—and her doom—approached. Flinging herself from the beach into the waves, she turned that instant into sea foam.

But that is not the end of her story—oh, no! Because little mermaid had refused to do such an evil deed, she was granted the chance to win a soul of her own by doing 300 years of good deeds. And as a child now of the air, not the sea, she went forward, happily, to win her place in the stars. ⭐

Seaweed Stuffed Shells

Good enough for the kings' daughters on land or sea. (Makes 4–5 servings)

Shells

 EQUIPMENT:

- large pot

- colander

- slotted spoon

 INGREDIENTS:

- water

- ¼ cup vegetable oil (60 ml)

- jumbo pasta shells (about 15)

DIRECTIONS:

1. Fill the large pot one-half to three-quarters with water.

2. Add the oil and bring to a boil at high temperature.

3. When the water boils, put pasta shells into the water carefully so as not to splash hot water on yourself.

4. Make sure shells are under water, then reduce to medium-high heat, boiling for the amount of time indicated on the box. Stir every once in a while to make sure the shells don't stick together.

5. Pour or spoon shells into the colander in the sink to drain.

*Facts about pasta:
1. The word "pasta" means paste in Italian. Its two essential ingredients are flour and water. 2. The Chinese had noodle-like food in 3000 BCE. Popular legend says that Marco Polo brought pasta to Italy in the late thirteenth century. However, there is evidence of a pasta dish in Italy in the fourth century BCE and evidence of macaroni for 2,000 years before that. Some scholars believe pasta actually began in the Arab countries.*

Filling

EQUIPMENT:

- steamer
- colander
- measuring cup
- measuring spoons
- large bowl
- large spoon

INGREDIENTS:

- 15 oz. container of ricotta cheese (28 g)
- 1 egg
- ½ tsp. salt
- ¼ tsp. pepper
- 1 tbsp. parsley
- ½ cup dry grated parmesan cheese (110 g)
- 1 bunch spinach (for seaweed!) or a 10 oz. (280 g) frozen package
- 2 cups shredded mozzarella cheese (225 g)

DIRECTIONS:

1. Steam the fresh spinach until wilted (only about 1 minute) or follow the directions on the frozen spinach to thaw. Drain in the colander and rinse with cold water. Press with the back of a spoon to get out as much water as possible. Set aside.

3. Greek mythology tells of the god Vulcan inventing strings of dough— early spaghetti?
4. English settlers brought pasta to the New World. Thomas Jefferson is said to have carried the very first macaroni-making machine to America from France in 1879, where he had served as an ambassador.
5. In 1740, in Venice, Italy, the first pasta factory opened. The first American pasta factory started in Brooklyn in 1848, where the spaghetti was spread out on the roof to dry in the sun.

2. Mix the ricotta and egg in the large bowl.

3. Measure the salt, pepper, parsley, and dry parmesan cheese, then mix into the ricotta and egg mixture.

4. Mix in the spinach.

5. Add ¾ cup (85 g) of the shredded mozzarella cheese into the ricotta mixture. Set aside or cover and refrigerate.

Tomato Sauce

You can use canned or bottled sauce for this recipe, or your family's recipe for homemade sauce. If you don't have a family recipe you can start with this one and make it your own by adding the spices you like best (maybe substituting oregano for the basil), experimenting with the kinds of tomatoes or amounts of garlic, or adding sautéed mushrooms and peppers.

EQUIPMENT:

• large pot

• large bowl

• colander with very small holes—metal or wire mesh work best

• slotted spoon

• sharp knife

• cutting board

• large pot or skillet

• spatula or large spoon

• measuring spoons

INGREDIENTS:

• 5 large, very ripe tomatoes

• ice and water

• 3 cloves of garlic, peeled and minced or pressed

• 2 tbsp. fresh basil, chopped

• 1 tsp. Italian herbs

• 6 oz. (168 ml) can of tomato paste (optional)

DIRECTIONS:

1. Fill a large pot halfway and set it to boil on high heat. Set the slotted spoon by the stove. Fill a large bowl three quarters of the way with ice and water and place it by the stove, too.

2. When the water boils, place each tomato into the pot with the slotted spoon and leave them in for 30 seconds, until the skin splits. Lift each back out and into the bowl of ice water with the slotted spoon, to stop the cooking process.

3. Let them cool and place the tomatoes on the cutting board.

4. Dump out the ice and water and place the colander in the bowl.

5. Peel the skin away from each tomato and discard the skin.

6. Cut each tomato into quarters, cutting out and discarding the core.

7. With your hands, squeeze the tomatoes into the colander catching the seeds in the colander and the juice in the bowl.

8. Chop the tomato pieces and put them, the juice, the minced or pressed garlic, the chopped basil, and the Italian herbs into a skillet or pot and bring to a boil. Lower the heat to medium. Cook for 30 minutes, stirring occasionally.

9. If the sauce seems too thin, add a can of tomato paste.

Assembling the Shells

EQUIPMENT:

- square 9x9 baking dish

- 2 spoons

- aluminum foil

1. Preheat oven to 375 degrees F (190 C).

2. Spoon a layer of sauce into the bottom of the baking dish.

3. Fill each pasta shell overflowing with the ricotta mixture and set in the baking dish. Set the next one close, even a little squished.

4. When the pan is full, spoon more sauce over the shells.

5. Cover with the remaining mozzarella cheese.

6. Cover the pan with foil and bake for 20 minutes.

7. Uncover and bake for another 5–10 minutes, until the sauce and cheese are bubbling.

8. Remove from oven and let sit for ten minutes before serving.

HODJA BORROWS A POT

One day, one fine day, Hodja decided to make kebabs for his family, but he didn't have the right pot for the rice. So off he went to his cousin's to borrow a big copper pot.

"Bring it back first thing in the morning," said his cousin, who did not trust Hodja at all. He was *such* a fool.

But first thing in the morning, Hodja was back with the big pot and there was a little pot inside of it.

"What's this? What's this?" asked the cousin.

Hodja grinned and struck his forehead with the flat of his hand. "Indeed, I am such a fool. I have forgotten to congratulate you. Your big pot has given birth to a little pot. Allah's blessings."

His cousin laughed, loud and long. What a fool Hodja was! "Thank you for your congratulations and may Allah bless you, too." Then his cousin took both pots into her kitchen.

• • •

This Turkish tale is typical of many of the short, pithy jest stories featuring the wise fool known as Hodja or Nasr-ed-Din Hodja. (The word "hodja" in old Turkey simply meant a Moslem scholar and teacher.) He can also be found in stories throughout the Middle East, where he is also called Jawha or Goha.

Some scholars believe there was an actual man named Hodja about whom these stories were told. In 1960 the Turkish government published an official collection of Nasr-ed-Din Hodja stories, and there is a government sanctioned tombstone for him at Akeshehiz, with the date 1284.

Not a week later, Hodja came back to borrow the big pot once again and, of course, hoping for another increase, the cousin loaned it to him.

"Bring it back first thing in the morning," she reminded him.

But Hodja did not bring the pot back that morning, nor the next, nor the next. A week went by, then two, and finally, exasperated, Hodja's cousin knocked on his door.

When Hodja answered, she shook her finger in his face. "Where is my pot? It is my best pot and I have friends coming to visit."

Hodja tore at his hair. "Alas," he cried, "I feared to tell you. It is so sad. The very night I borrowed your poor cauldron—Allah's ways are not to be questioned—the pot died!"

"Died?" cried the cousin. "How can you say such a thing? A pot cannot die."

Hodja smiled sweetly. "If a pot can give birth," he said, "then surely it can die."

Not such a fool after all, was Nasr-ed-Din Hodja. ⭐

This particular story has numerous variations. The one in Syria stars Djuha. In the Israeli version, a rabbi makes a ruling between cousins, one of whom has borrowed spoons and goblets, then a watch, which he claims has died. In India, the story is about a large balance of iron, which has presumably been eaten by mice.

Hodja's Kebabs

If you want rice, don't lend your cousin your pot. (Serves a family)

Yogurt Marinade

 EQUIPMENT:

- medium bowl
- garlic press
- spoon

INGREDIENTS:

- 1 cup plain yogurt (230 ml)
- 1 clove of garlic, pressed
- ½ tsp. salt
- ¼ tsp. pepper
- ¼ tsp. cumin

Lemon Marinade

 EQUIPMENT:

*Same as
Yogurt Marinade*

 INGREDIENTS:

- Juice from 1–2 lemons
  (approximately ½ cup
  or 115 ml)
- ½ cup olive oil (115 ml)
- 2 cloves of garlic, pressed
- 1 tsp. salt
- ¼ tsp. pepper

Facts about kebab:
*1. A kebab is a dish
of meat, and
sometimes vegetables,
that are roasted on
skewers.*
*2. The word
"kebab" comes from
the Arabic* kabb,
*which means cooked
meat in small pieces,
or possibly from the
Aramaic* kabb
*meaning burning or
charring.*
3. Shish-kebab
*consists of cubes of
meat like lamb, beef,
or chicken grilled on
skewers.* Adana
kebab *is spicy meat
patties on skewers,*
doner kebab *is the
Greek gyro,* tandir
kebab *is pit-roasted
lamb.*

DIRECTIONS:

1. Chose a marinade.

2. Mix all ingredients in a bowl.

Meat

EQUIPMENT:

• plastic wrap

• skewers

• broiler pan or grill

INGREDIENTS:

• chicken, lamb, beef, or shrimp

• vegetables such as peppers, onions, mushrooms, and tomatoes (optional)

DIRECTIONS:

1. Choose chicken, lamb, beef, or shrimp.

2. Clean and cut meat into cubes; de-vein and peel shrimp.

3. Add to marinade of choice, cover with plastic wrap and refrigerate for at least 1 hour.

4. Put meat on skewer, alternating with vegetables if you wish.

5. Cook on the grill or approximately 4 inches under the broiler on broiler pan (to catch juices away from kebabs) for 4–6 minutes

4. Kebab is essentially a Turkish dish that goes back to the time when the Turks were nomads grilling meat over campfires. The kebab spread through the Arab and Greek worlds.
5. In Turkey, an inexpensive kebab restaurant is called a kebabci.

per side for meat or until cooked to desired doneness. Chicken should be cooked entirely with no pink left in the middle. Check by cutting open a middle piece. Beef or lamb can be left pink in the middle and is a personal choice by the eater. For shrimp, cook 1½–2 minutes or until pinkish in color.

Serve with rice or with flat bread and vegetables.

Try adding Cucumber Yogurt Salad to complete the meal.

Cucumber Yogurt Salad

EQUIPMENT:

• medium bowl

• garlic press

• spoon

INGREDIENTS:

• ½ cup plain yogurt (115 ml)

• 2 cucumbers, peeled and cut lengthwise then chopped in thick semi-circles

• salt to taste

• 1 tsp. fresh chopped mint

• 1 garlic clove, pressed (optional)

DIRECTIONS:

Mix all ingredients in bowl and refrigerate until ready to serve.

THE THREE LEMONS

Once there was a king with only one son. For many years the prince refused to marry. But one day, when the prince was cutting apart a cream tart, he accidentally sliced his finger. A single drop of his blood fell into the cream and he was suddenly seized with the desire to find a wife who was as white as cream and red as blood.

The king was so pleased that his son was finally willing to marry, he gave his blessing. "Go, my boy. Find your heart's desire."

So off rode the prince, through farmyards and villages, along coastlines and up into the high mountains, looking for such a girl.

At last he came upon an old woman sitting under a tree, with a basket of fruit and cakes by her side. Being a polite young man, the prince inquired if she were just resting or needed help.

"Neither, dear boy, I have been waiting for you," she said. "Tell me why you wander so far from home."

So he told her his story, and when he was done, she presented him with three lemons. "As you were kind to me, I shall help you get your heart's desire. Go home, and along your way stop at the

This Italian story can be found all over Europe.

A similar Norwegian tale, with the same name, stars three brothers instead of a single prince, and a hag, plus a swarm of trolls instead of the one old lady. The girls in the lemons are not fairies, but princesses. And the serving girl is a cook. But the story itself remains the same.

very first well you see. There cut one of these lemons in half. A fairy will come out of it and ask for water. You must get it at once or she will disappear. The same with the second lemon, and the third. Do not let the third fairy disappear for she will be the wife of your heart."

The prince was delighted, and he bid the old wise woman farewell, then started for home.

• • •

It was not a day or three before he came to a well that was in a lovely copse of trees. There he dismounted and took out the first of the three lemons. With his knife, he sliced through the lemon and—in a flash—a beautiful girl appeared, as white as cream and with lips as red as strawberries.

"I need a drink of water!" she cried.

The prince was so dazzled by her that he was slow to do as she asked and, in an instant, she was gone.

So he reached into his saddlebag and took out the second lemon, then cut it open. A second fairy, more beautiful than the first, came out and demanded a drink. But once again the prince was slow and she, too, disappeared.

The prince knew that he dared not lose the third fairy, so this time he drew the water up from the well first. Then he cut open the final lemon, and when the third fairy appeared, he was ready and handed her a ladle-full of water.

When she had drunk her fill, the fairy turned to the prince and said, "Now, my prince, we shall be wed."

He could not believe his happiness. "Let me go home and return with an escort worthy of you, to lead you in splendor to my father's palace."

The fairy agreed and as soon as the prince was out of sight, she climbed into the fork of a tree overlooking the well so that she could watch all that happened but could not, herself, be seen.

No sooner had she climbed the tree than a hideous girl, the daughter of a mean mother and a meaner father, arrived at the well with a jar that needed filling. The girl was so ugly, her nose and chin threatened to meet in the middle and she had hardly three hairs on the top of her head.

As she leaned over the well, she saw reflected in it the face of the fairy in the tree. Now the hideous girl had never seen herself in any mirror, for her parents refused to have them in the house, and she thought the face was her own. Aloud she said, "Why Caramella, you are beautiful and should not be made to work a day longer."

Then she broke her mother's jar and capered around it. She looked so peculiar doing that, the fairy in the tree began to laugh.

Caramella glanced up and saw the fairy. In that instance, she realized the face she had seen in the well had been this beautiful creature's, not her own. Suddenly fearing she would be beaten by

Related to the "Forgotten Fiancee" stories (type 884) this tale has relatives in the folk music world as well. The song "The Nut Brown Maiden" is the story of a prince being duped into marrying the wrong girl.

In every instance of the tale, the deception is found out, the bad girl punished, and the princess/fairy finally returned to her proper position.

her mother for breaking the jar, Caramella said slyly: "Why are you in the tree, pretty maiden?"

The fairy saw no reason not to tell her. In that instant, Caramella decided on a wicked plan. "Let me comb your hair so that when the prince returns, you will be more beautiful than before."

The fairy agreed and climbed down. But while Caramella combed her hair, she struck the fairy with a pointed shard of the jar, to kill her. The moment the shard touched the fairy's head she cried out, "Dove!" and turned into a snow-white bird. Then she flew away over the trees and out of sight.

• • •

Soon after, the prince returned with his escort. Imagine his surprise when he was greeted by the hideous Caramella who said, "Oh, my prince, I am indeed the fairy from the third lemon, but I have been enchanted by a wizard into this awful form."

The prince felt that he was to blame, having left his beloved behind, so he took the ugly girl home, dressed in the splendid bridal clothes he had brought with him.

His father the king and his mother the queen did not dare say a word against Caramella for she was their son's choice of a bride.

A great wedding was planned, and every king and queen from far and wide was invited.

Now, as the cook was preparing the wedding feast, a snow-white dove with a red beak flew into the window and cried:

Alas, the prince and the false bride are wed,

While lives the true bride, both white and red.

The cook ran and told the king and queen who told the prince. The prince came into the kitchen and caught the white bird. As soon as he touched it, the bird turned back into the fairy, who told him how the hideous Caramella had tried to murder her.

"Wait here," he said, "behind the curtain." Then he returned to the wedding feast and addressed his guests. "What," he asked, "should be done to someone who tries to kill my beloved bride?"

They shouted out horrible punishments. "Such a one should be stoned!" And "Put in a barrel filled with vipers!" But Caramella said, "Burn her to death and scatter the ashes to the four winds."

The prince nodded. "You have pronounced your own death, wicked girl," he said. And it was done.

Then the prince married his real bride, whom he found in a lemon, and they lived happily ever after. ⭐

Lemon Chicken

No fairies in this lemon dish, but no sour puss either. (Makes 3–4 servings)

Facts about lemons:
1. The lemon is the berry of its tree.
2. The lemon fruit is actually green and not particularly sour. For lemons to become yellow and tart, the tree must grow where temperatures dip below 50 degrees F (10 degrees C) but always remain above freezing.
3. A lemon has 18 calories, and no fat or cholesterol, as well as 35 percent of the daily recommendation of Vitamin C.

EQUIPMENT:

- measuring spoons
- small bowl
- spoon
- cutting board
- sharp knife
- measuring cup (heat proof)
- large skillet or electric skillet with a top
- spatula

INGREDIENTS:

- 4 tbsp. butter (half stick) (60 g)
- 3 boneless, skinless chicken split breasts
- 2 tbsp. flour
- 1 tsp. tarragon
- 1 cube chicken bouillon dissolved in ¾ cup hot water (175 ml) (or ¾ cup stock)
- 1 lemon

DIRECTIONS:

1. Rinse the chicken in cool water.

2. Cut the chicken lengthwise into 1-inch (2.5 cm) strips.

3. Mix the flour and tarragon in the small bowl. Set aside.

4. Slice the lemon into thin slices. Discard the ends. Set aside.

5. Melt butter in the skillet at medium-high heat.

6. Place chicken into skillet and, while cooking, sprinkle a small spoonful of the flour/tarragon mixture on top of the chicken.

7. Mix with spatula constantly to coat and cook it evenly.

8. Sprinkle more flour/tarragon and repeat until all is in the pan and the chicken is cooked through.

9. Reduce heat to low.

10. Pour water/bouillon mixture over the chicken.

11. Top with lemons and cover. Let simmer for a minute.

12. Stir once and cover again, cooking for another minute or two.

13. Pour or spoon the entire dish onto a serving platter, slowly so as not to splash the juice and burn yourself.

SERVING SUGGESTIONS:

Try serving lemon chicken with Caesar Salad, rice, and garlic bread.

4. Scholars believe that the lemon originated in China, Persia, or the Indus Valley. By the second century, lemons were exported from Libya to Rome. We know this because a mosaic in the ruins of the city of Pompeii shows a lemon.

5. The ladies of Louis XIV's court in France used lemons to redden their lips.

6. The rind of the lemon is called the zest. It holds tiny sacs of lemon oil, and can be used in recipes.

Caesar Salad

EQUIPMENT:

- salad bowl
- salad tongs

INGREDIENTS:

- romaine lettuce, washed and ripped
- Caesar dressing
- freshly grated parmesan cheese
- croutons

DIRECTIONS:

Toss lettuce with dressing and top with cheese and croutons.

THE GREAT TURNIP

Once in old Russia, Grandfather planted a turnip. The turnip grew and grew and grew some more. It grew until it was huge, the size of a pot.

Grandfather came out of the house, puffing on his pipe. He tried to pull the turnip out. He pulled and pulled but the great turnip would not come out of the ground.

"Grandmother," he called, "help me pull this great turnip out of the ground for it is huge, the size of a pot."

So Grandmother came out of the house, a babushka on her head. She put her arms around Grandfather's waist and they pulled and they pulled but the great turnip would not come out of the ground.

Grandmother called to her daughter, "Masha, come and help us pull this great turnip out of the ground for it is huge, the size of a pot."

So Masha came out of the house, wiping her hands on her apron. She put her arms around Grandmother's shoulders and Grandmother had her arms around Grandfather's waist, and

This shaggy turnip story, motif Z49.9, comes from Russia, though versions of it have also been found in various of the Baltic states and in Scandinavia as well. I have added a few Russian names to my telling, but have otherwise left the story alone.

they pulled and they pulled but the great turnip would not come out of the ground.

Masha called to her dog, "Sasha, come out here and help us pull this great turnip out of the ground for it is huge, the size of a pot."

Then out came the dog, shaking his ears. He grabbed the ties on Masha's apron and Masha put her arms around Grandmother's shoulders and Grandmother had her arms around Grandfather's waist, and they pulled and they pulled but the great turnip would not come out of the ground.

Sasha barked to the cat, "Mischa, come out here and help us pull this great turnip out of the ground for it is huge, the size of a pot."

Then out came the cat, preening his whiskers. He grabbed the dog's tail and the dog grabbed the ties on Masha's apron and Masha put her arms around Grandmother's waist and Grandmother had her arms around Grandfather's waist, and they pulled and they pulled but the great turnip would not come out of the ground.

Mischa meowed to the mouse, "Kasha, come out here and help us pull this great turnip out of the ground for it is huge, the size of a pot."

Out came to the mouse, eating a piece of cheese, and she pulled on the cat's tail, and the cat grabbed the dog's tail and the dog grabbed the ties on Masha's apron and Masha put her arms around Grandmother's shoulders and Grandmother had her arms around Grandfather's waist, and they pulled and they pulled.

Kasha pulled Mischa, Mischa pulled Sasha, Sasha pulled Masha, Masha pulled Grandmother, Grandmother pulled Grandfather and the huge turnip. . . .came out of the ground. Then they all went inside the house and had turnip for dinner. ⭐

This is a familiar cumulative tale, the kind of story especially popular with the youngest story lovers. It is often told in kindergartens, with all the children joining in. Almost like a game, cumulative tales invite the listener to recite along with them. Think of "This is House that Jack Built" and "The Gingerbread Man." They are cumulative stories as well.

Mashed Turnips

You can work up quite an appetite with all that pulling. (Serves a family)

EQUIPMENT:
- cutting board
- sharp knife
- medium-sized pan
- colander
- measuring cup
- bowl
- potato masher or electric mixer

INGREDIENTS:
- 1 large or 4 small turnips
- ⅛ cup milk (30 ml)
- stick of butter (115 g) (though you can use less)
- ½ tsp. salt
- ⅛ tsp. pepper
- extra salt for boiling water

DIRECTIONS:

1. Peel and cut turnip(s) into 1-inch (2.5 cm) by 3-inch (7 cm) strips.

2. Put the turnip pieces in a pan and cover with water. Add a dash of salt and bring to a boil; then reduce heat to medium high.

3. Boil for approximately 30 minutes, until the turnips are tender (can be checked with a fork).

144

4. Put the colander in the sink, then pour out the turnips and water into it. Rinse with hot tap water.

5. In the bowl, mash the turnips, butter, milk, salt, and pepper by hand with the potato masher or with the electric mixer.

6. When done, it will still be lumpy.

IF YOU DON'T HAVE TURNIPS, TRY THESE OTHER MASHED TUBERS:

Mashed Potatoes

Follow the same directions with 5 or 6 large potatoes. Use only half a stick of butter and potatoes may need more milk, so start with the ⅛ cup (30 ml) and add a little more at a time as needed. When done, they will be smooth.

Mashed Yams or Butternut Squash:

Follow the same directions with 4 large yams or 1 or 2 butternut squash. You will need to remove the seed and stringy middle from the squash. Use only half a stick of butter and no milk. Add 1–2 tablespoons of brown sugar. 🍅

4. The turnip, with its whitish hue, is closely related to the yellow rutabaga or swede (Brassica napo-brassica.)
5. Since turnips thrive in cold, damp climates, they became the poor people's main meal until potatoes came along.
6. At one time in Europe, throwing a turnip at someone was considered a great insult.

JACK AND THE BEANSTALK

Long ago, a poor woman lived in a remote village. Her husband had been killed years earlier and all his money taken, so she and her son Jack lived in poverty in a small cottage.

Now one day even the cow stopped giving milk so there was nothing to do but sell it. So the woman called her son and said, "Jack, take Bossy to market and get the very best you can for her. Without money, we will surely starve."

So Jack took the cow and they went along and they went along until they met a strange man on the road.

"Where are you going, Jack?" asked the man, and indeed it was strange that he knew Jack's name.

"I am going to market to sell our cow," said Jack. "For without a good price for her, my mother and I shall surely starve."

"I have just the thing," said the man and he took off his hat and shook something into his hand. "Magic beans," he said showing them to Jack. "Nothing better."

So Jack gave him the cow and went home well satisfied with his trade. But when he told his mother what he had exchanged for the cow, she put her apron up over her head and wept. "Jack,

The publishing history of this particular tale begins with a tract called "Round about our Coal-Fire" printed in London in 1730. The story of "Jack Spriggins and the Enchanted Bean" is only a chapter in it. Seventy years later, the story was published by itself as "The History of Mother Twaddle, and The Marvelous Achievements of Her Son Jack."

Jack, those beans are worthless." She took them from him and flung them out of the window. Then they both went to bed hungry.

• • •

But the beans were magic! During the night they grew and grew into a tall beanstalk. When Jack woke up, he saw the beanstalk out of his window, thick as a cow's middle and green as a fairy's coat. He jumped up and ran out to the garden. The beanstalk formed a kind of ladder that ran right up into the sky.

"If I climb up," Jack thought, "perhaps I will find my fortune there." But being a good boy, he first went back to tell his mother.

Well, she begged and pleaded for him to stay at home. "You will break my heart, and your head besides," she said.

"But Mother, if I have done wrong by selling the cow for a handful of beans, surely I will do right by finding where the magic beanstalk leads."

"Magic is not for the likes of us," she said. "It was the death of your father. He had some bits and pieces of magic, and was killed for them."

Well, it was the first Jack had ever heard of this. He thought his father had been killed by thieves. Still, ignoring his mother's pleas, he went out to the garden again and began to climb. It took hours, and of course Jack was starving, having missed dinner the night before and all the meals that day. But still he went up and up and up, until the earth below him was obscured by clouds.

And then, quite suddenly, he reached the top, where the beanstalk spread out like a path. The path turned into a road. The road into a highway. Soon Jack saw before him an enormous house.

Standing before the door of the house was the tallest woman Jack had ever seen, clearly five times his size. Why, he barely came up to her knee, and him almost a man.

"Go away, boy!" she called when she noticed him. "For my husband is a giant and he eats the flesh of humans. Why, he is off right now scouring the countryside for any meat he can find."

The idea of this giantess's husband quite terrified Jack, but he had been climbing all day without a bite to eat or a sip of water. He was tired and frantic and knew he had not the strength to turn around and go home.

"Please hide me, for just one night," he begged, "and I will be gone at first light."

Well, the good woman—for though she was a giantess, she had a fine heart—agreed. She fed him and gave him plenty to drink as well. Then she hid him in the oven. And just in time. For no sooner had Jack curled up to sleep for the night, then her husband returned, calling out,

> Fe, fi, fo, fum,
> I smell the blood of an Englishman.
> Be he alive or be he dead,
> I'll grind his bones to make my bread.

There are many Jack stories, in both British and American folklore. In them, Jack is the hero, the trickster, and sometimes the fool as well.

The famous rhyme said by the giant actually differs from story to story. Instead of

> Be he alive
> or be he dead
> I'll grind his bones
> to make my bread,

one American version ends:

> I'll grind his bones
> To eat with my
> pones.

149

Jack's teeth began to rattle, his knees to knock. He peeked out through a crack in the oven door.

The giantess answered, "What you smell are the humans in the dungeon, dear."

So the giant sat down at the kitchen table and said, "Bring me my hen and my harp." And as soon as his wife brought the hen and the harp, the giant picked them both up and said:

> *Lay, hen, lay,*
> *Play, harp, play,*
> *Ease me through*
> *This difficult day.*

No sooner had the giant said these words then the hen laid a golden egg and the harp began to play by itself, a tune so wonderfully soothing, that the giant fell immediately to sleep and began to snore. And beside him his wife slept, too.

Quickly, quietly, Jack opened the oven door, picked up the little hen, and stuffed it into his pocket. He grabbed up the singing harp and slung it over his shoulder. Then he found a great key on a rack and went down to the dungeon, where he freed all of the people who were destined to be the giant's supper. After that, he sneaked outside.

But no sooner was he out, then the hen began to cackle and the harp began to sing, "Master! Master!"

The giant awoke and started toward the door. Jack could hear his great feet slamming against the floor.

So Jack ran to the beanstalk. Then hand over hand, with the hen flapping about in his pocket and the harp singing out for help, he began to climb down.

The giant came fast behind him, the beanstalk shaking with his weight.

When Jack neared the bottom, he cried out, "Mother, Mother, quick fetch me Father's ax!"

She did just that and the minute Jack's feet touched the good earth, he chopped away at the beanstalk until he had chopped clean through. The beanstalk fell over and the giant hit the ground so hard, he died in an instant.

When Jack showed the hen and harp to his mother, she was not surprised. "Why, that is your father's own hen that lays golden eggs and the harp that soothes a hurting heart. I never thought to find them again, not after the giant stole what was ours."

So Jack and his mother never had to worry about money again, nor the countryside about giants. And everyone lived quite happily ever after. Except, of course, the giant. ⭐

Jack's Magic Party Beans

No humans were harmed in the making of this recipe, and still it's hearty enough for a giant. (Makes enough for a party)

EQUIPMENT:

- sharp knife
- cutting board
- frying pan
- spatula
- tongs
- paper towels on a plate
- colander (optional)
- crock-pot or large pot
- can opener
- measuring spoons
- measuring cup
- large spoon

INGREDIENTS:

- 1 package or 1 pound bacon (450 g)
- 1 pound ground beef (450 g)
- ½ onion, chopped
- 1½ tsp. dried mustard
- ¼ cup catsup (60 ml)
- 3 tbsp. black strap molasses
- ¾ cup dark brown sugar (150 g)
- Beans: 3–8 cans of several varieties such as pork and beans, navy, white, and kidney

DIRECTIONS:

1. Cut the bacon into inch-long (2.5 cm) strips and place in the frying pan. Fry over medium heat, moving the bacon occasionally with the spatula, until completely cooked and crispy. When done, remove the bacon from the pan with tongs and place on top of a plate covered with paper towels to soak the grease out.

2. Pour off the grease from the pan when it is cooled a bit (so as not to spatter and burn yourself) and put the ground beef and the chopped onion in the frying pan to cook. Cook over medium high heat until all the beef is brown. Pour off the grease or pour everything into a colander.

3. Put the drained beef and onion mixture and the bacon into the large pot and set the heat to medium. Or, in the crock-pot, set to low for all-day cooking.

4. Open and drain the cans of beans.

5. Add the mustard, catsup, vinegar, molasses, dark brown sugar, and the beans to the pot.

6. Cook this dish until heated through, or leave on low in the crock-pot until time to serve.

4. Broad beans and soybeans originated in Europe, but the rest were originally grown in the Americas by the native peoples. The common bean is believed to have first been cultivated in southern Mexico and Central America over 7,000 years ago.
5. The Greeks and Romans used the broad bean for voting. The white seeds meant agreement; the black seeds disagreement.
6. While beans are easy to grow, they are also easily susceptible to diseases like rusts, blights, and wilts.

153

These beans are fabulous for a cookout served with hot dogs and hamburgers or with barbecued chicken or ribs. Make a large batch in the crock-pot and cook all day for a party. For a really large party—or a giant—just add more beans.

VARIATIONS:

For vegetarians, this recipe can be made without the bacon and beef.

Try substituting ground turkey for the ground beef. Or, you can use just one of the meats instead of both.

Any beans can be used in this recipe. Try different kinds to change the taste.

DESSERTS

CINDERELLA
Pumpkin Tartlets

THE MAGIC PEAR TREE
Magic Pear Grumble

SNOW WHITE
Snow White's Baked Apples

SEVEN HILLS OF SWEET
Sweet Chocolate Mousse

CINDERELLA

Once there was a man of some property and means whose wife had died, leaving him with a young daughter named Ella.

Believing the child needed a mother to raise her, he married soon after, a woman with two daughters of her own. But hardly were the wedding vows spoken then the new wife began to show her bad temper. She made Ella clean the dishes and mop the floors and do all the work in the house. Ella was even thrown out of her own bedroom and given a straw pallet in the attic. If her father noticed anything, he said nothing for he was ruled entirely by his new wife.

Each day, after she had finished her many chores, little Ella would sit and sigh by the fire, where her clothes became dirty with the cinders. Because of this, her two stepsisters began calling her Cinderella. They pointed their fingers and laughed at her, never realizing that with all their finery, they were not half as beautiful as the poor girl in the ashes.

• • •

Now it happened that the king's son gave a great ball and everyone who was anyone in society was invited, including Cinderella's stepmother and stepsisters. So on top of all her other chores, Cinderella now had to iron their new dresses and touch up the laces and clean their diamonds and shine their silver baubles.

As she was helping the sisters into their gowns and combing their hair, one of them said, "Cinderella, I wager you would like to go to the ball," while the other laughed at the thought.

Of course Cinderella longed to go, but how could she? She had neither dress nor shoes, nor coach to take her. So when they all left, in a flurry of finery, in a coach pulled by four matched horses, she waved sadly, then went back into the house and sat down by the fire to weep.

She cried, "If only I could go to the ball, I should never ask for anything more."

Suddenly, her godmother, who was a fairy—with wings and a wand and who knew a wish when she heard it—appeared before her, wrapped in stars. "Will you work for your wish, my dear?"

Cinderella scrubbed away the tears with the back of her hand, and nodded.

"Then go into the garden and get me a pumpkin," said her fairy godmother.

Gladly, Cinderella did as she was asked and when she returned, the fairy had her scoop out the insides of the pumpkin. When that was done, the fairy touched the pumpkin with her wand and it turned into a splendid coach, gilded all over.

Then Cinderella was sent to the mousetrap where she found six grey mice and her fairy godmother struck each one in turn and they became grey horses to pull the coach.

"But what shall we do for a coachman?" mused the fairy.

"I know where there's a rat in the rat-trap," said Cinderella and quickly went to fetch him, and he became a round, jolly coachman.

Then six green lizards were found who became footmen, their liveries as green as their skins had been.

"Get in, get in," cried the fairy, "there's no time to waste."

"But I cannot go dressed like this," Cinderella pointed out sensibly, "for I should never be let in."

So her godmother touched the wand to Cinderella's raggedy dress and it turned into cloth of gold and silver, with loops of diamonds and pearls cunningly worked along the bodice and hem. Right after that, the godmother touched Cinderella's bare feet and she was suddenly shod in glass slippers, as fine as any shoe in the most elegant shop.

"Now go and dance until midnight," said the fairy, "but be certain you leave when the bells strike the hour, for the magic will fail at the last stroke and you will have only a pumpkin, six mice, six lizards, and a rat to bring you home."

The three elements in all the Cinderella stories are: the girl deprived of her inheritance, the help of a magic maker, and the girl not allowed to reveal herself until she is recognized. In most tales there is no glass slipper; indeed in some there is no slipper at all. A few scholars feel that the glass slipper was a mistake on the part of either Charles Perrault, who set the tale down in French, or one of his translators, who mistook the word vair, *which means variegated fur, for* verre, *which means glass.*

161

Cinderella promised, "Oh I will, Godmother, I will," and away she went.

· · ·

When she got to the ball, Cinderella looked like a magnificent foreign princess. No one knew her. The prince himself led her into the hall and danced only with her. He was about to give her a kiss and tell her he wanted to marry her when the clock in the bell tower began striking midnight.

Suddenly remembering what would happen at the last stroke, Cinderella tore herself away from the prince. She ran out of the castle and down the stairs. As she reached the gate, the last bell tolled and her coach was gone, her dress in tatters. The guards who let her out thought she was some country maid who had gotten in by mistake. And all that was left behind was one of the glass slippers, which the prince found.

· · ·

Now when the stepsisters got home, they could only talk about the beautiful princess. Cinderella asked them to tell her more and, little suspecting, they did.

The next day, the prince sent around his royal coach with the glass slipper on a little pink cushion. He insisted that his valet let every young woman in the kingdom try the slipper on. "For I mean to marry the girl this glass slipper fits," he proclaimed.

So one by one the young women tried—big feet and little feet, fat feet and skinny feet—but the glass slipper fit none of them.

At last the prince's coach stopped before Cinderella's house. The two stepsisters tried on the shoes, but one had toes that were too big and one had a heel that was too large and neither could shove a foot into the slipper.

"Pray, let me try," begged Cinderella.

The two stepsisters laughed, but the valet pushed them aside. "My prince demands *every* young woman try," he said.

"She is just a cinder-maid," they protested, but the prince's valet insisted.

Of course, when he put the glass slipper on her foot, it went on with ease. The stepsisters were stunned, but even more stunned when Cinderella pulled the matching slipper from her pocket.

At that very moment, the fairy godmother appeared—wing, wand, and stars—and touched Cinderella's dress with magic, and suddenly she was even more magnificent than she had been at the ball.

Stepsisters and stepmother threw themselves at Cinderella's feet and begged for forgiveness and—for all the right reasons and none of the wrong ones—she did just that. Then she was escorted to the palace where the prince married her. Two days later, her stepsisters were married to two great lords of the court. And everyone really did live happily ever after. ⭐

Pumpkin Tartlets

What else would you do after midnight with a retired coach?

(Makes 40 tartlets)

EQUIPMENT:

- bowl
- can opener
- mixing spoon
- measuring cup
- measuring spoons
- food processor
- mini muffin tin
- 3-inch round cookie cutter or a drinking glass
- paper towel
- toothpick

INGREDIENTS:

Filling:
- 1 15-oz. can of pumpkin (450 g)
- ½ cup evaporated milk (115 ml)
- 2 eggs
- ½ cup brown sugar (100 g)
- ½ cup sugar (100 g)
- 1 tsp. cinnamon
- ¼ tsp. ginger
- ¼ tsp. ground cloves
- ¼ tsp. nutmeg

Topping:
- ¼ cup ground walnuts (40 g)
- ¼ cup brown sugar (50 g)
- 1 tbsp. cold butter (12 g)

Crust:
- 4 pre-made pie crusts
- Butter to grease the muffin tin if it is not non-stick

Facts about pumpkins:
1. The word pumpkin comes from the Greek word pepon, *meaning large melon. (Indeed, it is not a vegetable, but a fruit.)*
2. Pumpkins originated in Central America, perhaps as far back as 5500 BCE. *The Native Americans ate pumpkin long before the Pilgrims landed.*
3. Pumpkins are healthy and contain potassium, beta-carotene, and Vitamin A. Once they were used as a cure for freckles and snakebite.

DIRECTIONS:

1. Preheat oven to 425 degrees F (220 C).

2. Mix all the filling ingredients in a bowl. Set aside.

3. Grind walnuts in the food processor. Add the brown sugar and butter cut into small pieces. Grind until crumbly.

4. If your mini muffin pan is not non-stick, butter the insides or spray lightly with cooking spray.

5. Lay out the pie crusts and cut them into rounds by placing the cookie cutter or drinking glass upside down and pushing down firmly. You should be able to get approximately 10 tartlet shells from each pie shell. They do not need to be perfectly round.

6. Gently press the rounds into the muffin tin. This is easier if you form them into a slight cup shape first so you don't poke a hole through them.

7. Put 1 tablespoon filling in each shell.

8. Sprinkle with 1 teaspoon of the topping.

9. Put the tartlets in the oven for 10 minutes.

4. The largest pumpkin ever grown weighed 1,140 pounds.
5. The largest pumpkin pie ever baked weighed over 350 pounds (160 kg). It used 80 pounds (36 kg) of cooked pumpkin and took six hours to bake.
6. Pumpkins are 90 percent water.

10. With the tartlets still in the oven, lower the temperature to 350 degrees F (175 C) and cook for 12–15 more minutes or until a toothpick can be stuck in and comes out clean.

11. Cool for 5–10 minutes before removing from the tin.

Pie crusts

You can, of course, make your own crusts, but cutting circles from the store bought crusts makes this an easy and delicious dessert.

THE MAGIC PEAR TREE

Long ago in China, a farmer brought his pears to the market in a hand-drawn cart. He was just setting up his stall when a Taoist priest, worn with care, came over to him.

"Please," said the priest, "may I have a piece of fruit. Just one old, bruised pear will do, I do not ask for more."

The farmer tried to get rid of him, but the priest would not leave. He held out his hand, begging for that one pear.

"I sell my fruit, I do not give them away," said the farmer angrily. "I do not like beggars, whether they are priests or poor men. Away with you."

Soon, of course, this argument drew a crowd. The crowd drew the guards. And finally, to disperse the crowd, one of the guards purchased a small pear and threw it to the priest.

The priest nodded and thanked the guard, then spoke to the crowd. "How hard it is to understand greed. Let me offer some pears to all of you. All I wanted was a seed for planting." He ate the pear but reserved the seed.

Now the people crowded around to see what he would do next.

Taking a little shovel that he had tied around his back, the priest dug a hole and planted the seed, covering it up with earth.

"Can someone bring me hot water?"

A cautious laugh ran around the crowd, but one small boy ran, got the water, and gave it to the priest who immediately poured it on the planted seed.

Suddenly a green shoot shot up from the dark earth. It grew and grew and grew some more until it became an enormous pear tree, bursting with blooms. Even as the people watched, the blooms became pears, golden and heavy.

The priest turned, plucked the pears, and distributed them to everyone in the crowd, saving two for the small boy who had run for the water.

Then taking his shovel, the priest chopped down the tree. When he was finished, he picked up the top half of the tree and walked down the road. The people watched until he was out of sight.

Immediately the crowd dispersed and the farmer, who had been watching all of this magical show with them, turned back to his cart to find it was entirely empty and the handle of his wagon had been chopped off as well.

"Hey!" he cried, looking around. But priest, handle, guards, crowd—and pears—were all gone and he was left with nothing. ⭐

Today, most people in the West would recognize Taoist priests from such Hong Kong movies as Crouching Tiger, Hidden Dragon.

The Chinese philosopher Lao-Tzu (c.604–521 BCE), summed up its tenets thus:

Look, and it can't be seen.
Listen, and it can't be heard.
Reach, and it can't be grasped.

Magic Pear Grumble

Cures the grumbling of even the hungriest belly. And the secret ingredient? Hot water to make it grow. (Serves a family)

<table>
<tr><td>

Facts about pears:
1. Pears have been part of the Asian diet for centuries. They traveled to Europe in the Middle Ages, and to America in 1620.
2. In the eighteenth century, pears were nicknamed "butter fruit" because of their soft texture.
3. The pear is actually a member of the rose family.

</td></tr>
</table>

EQUIPMENT:

- large bowl

- measuring cup

- measuring spoons

- wisk

- peeler

- knife

- small heat-proof bowl

- teakettle or pan to boil water

- rubber spatula

- 2-quart (2 liter) baking dish or casserole

INGREDIENTS:

- 1 cup flour (115 g)

- ⅔ cup sugar (265 g)

- 1½ tsp. baking powder

- ½ tsp. cinnamon

- ⅛ tsp. salt

- ⅛ tsp. ground cloves

- ½ cup milk (115 ml)

- 4 ripe pears, peeled, cored and cut into ½–¾ inch (1–2 cm) chunks

- ¾ cup packed light brown sugar (150 g)

- ¼ cup butter (55 g), cut into 5 pieces

- ¾ cup boiling water (175 ml)

172

DIRECTIONS:

1. Preheat the oven to 375 degrees F (190 C).

2. In the large bowl, using the whisk, mix together the flour, white sugar, baking powder, cinnamon, salt, and ground cloves until completely combined.

3. Add milk and beat until smooth. This batter will be very thick and sticky.

4. With the rubber spatula, fold in the pear chunks.

5. Scoop the batter into the ungreased baking dish or casserole.

6. Boil water and measure ¾ cup (175 ml). (If you put the correct amount of water on to boil, it will be less when it is hot.)

7. Put the butter and brown sugar into the small heat-proof bowl and pour the hot water over it. Stir until melted and blended.

8. Pour the hot water mixture over the batter in the baking dish/casserole—do not mix.

9. Bake for 45 minutes. The finished dessert will be still a little syrupy with golden brown bready tufts.

4. Of the more than 3,000 varieties of pears, the most popular is the Bartlett.
5. Pears are a healthy snack and a good source of Vitamin C and fiber.
6. Pears ripen better off the tree than on. Some experts even recommend putting them in a brown paper bag and leaving them at room temperature, to hasten ripening.

SERVING SUGGESTIONS:

Serve with vanilla ice cream or whipped cream, or both.

VARIATIONS:

Try making this dessert with apples (peel and cut 2 large apples into small bits).

Or with peaches (5 medium peaches—to peel, put peaches in boiling water for 30 seconds, then rinse them in very cold water or drop them in a bowl of ice water to stop the cooking, then peel and cut).

For a sweeter crumble, use 2 cups of canned fruit instead of fresh.

SNOW WHITE

Once in midwinter, the snow falling like feathers from the sky, a queen sat by her bedchamber window embroidering a piece of cloth. The frame of the window was dark ebony, night-black. The snow was an unblemished white. The queen accidentally pricked her finger with the needle and three drops of blood landed on the snow.

Time seemed to stop, the world ceased turning, the queen sighed. "I wish I had a child as white as snow, as red as blood, as black as wood."

Nine months later she gave birth to a daughter who was white as snow, with blood-red lips, and hair as black as ebony. Her father called her Snow White.

But when the child was born, the queen died, and all that followed was a consequence of wishing.

•　•　•

Worried that his daughter needed a mother and the kingdom needed a queen, the king married a year later. The woman was beautiful, but she was proud, haughty, cold as ice. She was an enchantress whose magic mirror spoke to her in the dead of the night.

1. *The main written source of this tale can be found in the Grimm's collection. The Grimm brothers got the tale from two sisters, Jeannette and Amalie Hassenpflug of Cassel.*
2. *The story has appeared with little variation from the British Isles to Asia Minor and even into Central Africa.*
3. *Earlier literary versions of the story can be found in* Il Pentamerone, *an Italian collection of stories, but they were never as popular as the Grimm tale.*

Often the new queen would look in the mirror and say:

> *"Mirror, mirror, on the wall,*
> *Who's the fairest of us all?"*

And the mirror would grow cloudy, then sharp, and reply:

> *"Answering you by your own demand—*
> *You are the fairest in the land."*

But Snow White was growing up, and she was a beautiful child. More beautiful, many said, than the queen.

• • •

One day when Snow White had turned thirteen years old, the queen asked her mirror the same question:

> *"Mirror, mirror, on the wall,*
> *Who's the fairest of us all?"*

This time the mirror grew cloudy, then sharp, and replied:

> *"That you are beautiful, queen, 'tis true,*
> *But Snow White is much more beautiful than you."*

The queen screamed and threw her hairbrush at the mirror. Luckily her aim was terrible and she hit the window instead, shattering it. She could not, however, as easily break the memory of what the mirror had said. Day and night, envy had her by the throat and gnawed at her.

At last she called her best huntsman to her.

"Take the child, Snow White, into the woods. Kill her and bring me her heart and liver as proof of what you have done."

The huntsman was terrified. "She is the king's daughter, majesty."

The queen drew herself up and her face was both beautiful and terrible at the same time. "I am the king's wife."

• • •

The huntsman knew that he had to obey. He went to Snow White and said he was to take her hunting. And eager to learn, Snow White went away with him.

But when they were in the deepest part of the forest, the huntsman drew his knife. "I am only obeying the queen's command, princess," he said.

"Oh huntsman, spare my life," Snow White cried, looking up at him with limpid eyes. "I shall run into the forest and never return."

He put away the knife. "Run away, child, run away!" And as soon as she was gone, he killed a young deer and cut out its heart and liver and brought it back to the wicked queen. He told her they belonged to the child.

The queen had the cook salt and cook the meat and ate it, savoring every bite.

• • •

Meanwhile in the woods, Snow White ran desperately on and on, over sharp stones, through sharper thorns, and into the dark of night. At last, exhausted, and cold, and frightened beyond measure, she came upon a little cottage in the woods. Without

4. In 1937, Walt Disney made a movie version of the story, basing it on the Grimm's telling, though he left out the ending where the witch must dance in red-hot iron shoes.
5. Snow White and the Seven Dwarfs was the first commercially successful TechniColor feature-length animated film. Until the Disney movie, the seven dwarfs did not have names or distinct personalities.

even knocking she went in and to her surprise the place was as neat and clean as a palace.

The table was set with seven places, and there were seven little beds neatly made at the back of the room. She tried one bed after another, but they were either too short or too long, too hard or too soft. At last, she crept onto the seventh bed and as it was just right, she fell fast asleep.

Not a minute later, the owners of the cottage came home. They were seven dwarfs who worked the mines. They looked around the house, smelling a strange human smell. And when they found Snow White, small and beautiful, they let her sleep. The seventh dwarf shared a bed one hour at a time with each of his companions until night was done.

· · ·

In the morning, Snow White awoke and found the little men awake before her. She told them of her troubles and how her wicked stepmother had tried to have her killed.

The little men said, "Stay here with us. We will protect you and you can be our sister. Keep the house neat while we work and have hot supper ready for us when we return and all will be well. But be sure never to let anyone come in while we are away."

"With all my heart," cried Snow White.

And so it was.

· · ·

Now the queen, believing that she had eaten Snow White's heart and liver, went to the mirror. And she asked gaily:

"Mirror, mirror, on the wall,

Who's the fairest of us all?"

The mirror grew cloudy, then sharp, and replied:

"You are beautiful, queen, tis true,

But Snow White in the forest is more beautiful than you."

"Snow White? She is dead!" cried the queen.

The mirror answered:

"Over the hill, where seven dwarfs dwell

Snow White still lives, beautiful and well."

The queen knew this had to be true, for the mirror was incapable of lying. So she had the huntsman put in the dungeon for deceiving her. Then she took out her basket of magical potions. She drank down one after another until she looked like a young peddler woman. In this disguise she went into the forest to find the house of the seven dwarfs.

The little cottage was neat and snug. Lights gleamed from the window. The peddler woman knocked on the door. "I have laces," she cried. "Pretty laces."

When Snow White looked out the window and saw her, she had no fear and invited the young woman in.

"May I try on the laces?" she asked.

"Of course, my pretty, said the peddler woman, but she laced

Snow White up so tightly, the girl could not breathe and fell down as if dead.

"Now I am the most beautiful," said the wicked queen with a laugh, and she raced home to the palace.

• • •

Not long after the dwarfs returned home, found Snow White, and cut the laces. As soon as Snow White returned to life again, she told them what had happened.

"That was no peddler—that was your stepmother in disguise," they said. "Never let anyone into the house."

Snow White promised, "With all my heart."

And so it was.

• • •

FAIRY TALE FEASTS: **Desserts**

But the queen, back in her palace, soon asked the mirror her question and was returned the same reply.

"You are beautiful, queen, tis true,

But Snow White in the forest is more beautiful than you."

What could she do but haul out her potions again. This time she disguised herself as a middle-aged peddler woman and carried with her a poisoned comb.

When she arrived at the cottage, and knocked at the door, Snow White looked out the window. "I can not let you in."

"Then you come out, dearie," said the peddler woman. And, as Snow White had not been warned against that, she did.

"Let me comb your hair and you will see how lovely this golden comb looks against your dark hair," said the peddler.

But no sooner had Snow White agreed, then the poison began its deadly work and in moments the girl lay senseless on the ground.

"Now I am the most beautiful," said the wicked queen with a laugh, and she raced home to the palace.

Fortunately it was almost dinner time and the dwarfs arrived home, took out the comb, and Snow White was once again saved.

• • •

Meanwhile in the palace, the queen learned once again that Snow White was still alive for the mirror told her:

"Over the hill, where seven dwarfs dwell
Snow White still lives, beautiful and well."

The queen shook with rage. She dragged out her basket of potions once more and drank down every one until she looked like an ancient crone. Taking a new fallen apple, green on one side, red on the other, she set a deadly poison in the red side but let the green side be. Then off she sped to the cottage with a basket full of apples, and the death-bearing one on the top.

This time Snow White was ever more cautious. "I cannot let you in, I cannot go outside."

"You need to do neither, my pretty," said the crone. "I just wish to give you my basket of apples so that you may cook seven little pies for your little men. And so you be not afraid of the apples, I will even eat of one." And she took a big bite out of the green side of the top apple. "I will leave them here for you." Then the old crone hobbled away.

•   •   •

As soon as she saw the old woman was away from the clearing, Snow White ventured outside. The apple, half eaten, looked so inviting—magic can tempt even the wary—that she picked it up and took a big bite of the red and luscious-looking side. The poisoned apple stuck in her throat and she fell down, dead.

The wicked queen came out from behind a tree where she had been hiding and she danced around the fallen girl. "Now I am the most beautiful." And with a laugh, she picked up the rest of the poisoned apple and raced home to the palace.

There she asked the mirror her question and the mirror answered:

> *"Answering you by your own demand—*
> *You are the fairest in the land."*

And the queen was satisfied at last.

• • •

When the dwarfs came home that evening and found Snow White lying cold and stiff on the ground, they could not find how she was poisoned, for they could not see the apple piece in her throat.

They were going to bury her, but she looked so beautiful—white and red and black—that they could not bear to shut her away in the earth. So they made a glass casket and set her at the crossroads with a sign marked with golden letters:

SHE IS A KING'S DAUGHTER AND A FRIEND.

• • •

Now it happened that a king's son had come through the woods with his hunting party and he found the glass casket and read the sign. And when he looked through the glass, Snow White was so beautiful and innocent that he fell in love right then.

"Let me take the casket home," he begged the dwarfs. "I will prize her above all others for the rest of my life."

So the dwarfs let him take the casket away but as his servants began lifting it, one of them stumbled over a tree stump. The bump jarred the bit of poisoned apple, which fell out of Snow White's mouth and with a sigh she lifted the lid of the coffin and sat up.

"Where am I?" she asked in wonder.

"With the man who loves you truly," replied the young prince.

• • •

So Snow White went with the prince to the kingdom across the mountain and became his bride.

Now the wicked stepmother and her husband the king were invited to the wedding, though they did not know who the bride was. The evil queen arrayed herself in her finest clothes and stood in front of her mirror and asked:

"Mirror, mirror, on the wall,

Who's the fairest of us all?"

The mirror grew cloudy, then sharp, and replied:

"You are beautiful, tis true,

But the new young queen is more beautiful than you."

The wicked woman could not believe this and went on to the wedding. When she got there, she recognized Snow White, and turned to leave, but it was too late. They had been waiting for her to arrive and the guards grabbed her by the arms and forced her into red hot iron slippers, which she had to dance in until she dropped down dead. ⭐

Snow White's Baked Apples

The fairest dessert of all. (Serves one person per apple)

EQUIPMENT:

- sharp knife
- fruit coring tool or a thin sharp knife
- cutting board
- small bowl
- measuring cup
- measuring spoons
- butter knife
- baking pan

INGREDIENTS:

- 1 apple per person, any kind, though red-skinned varieties hold up better
- ¼ cup sugar (50 g)
- 1 tbsp. cinnamon
- 1 heaping tbsp. raisins per apple
- 1 tbsp. butter per apple
- Juice: orange, apple, apple cider, or cranberry

DIRECTIONS:

1. Preheat oven to 350 degrees F (175 C).

2. Mix the cinnamon and sugar together in a small bowl.

3. Cut off the top and bottom of each apple–just a thin slice.

Facts about apples:
1. The apple was the most popular fruit of ancient Greeks and Romans. There is evidence of humans eating apples as early as 6500 BCE. The Romans probably introduced apples to much of Europe.
2. The science of apple growing is called pomology. There are now 7,500 varieties of apples grown throughout the world.
3. Apples are members of the rose family.

4. Core each apple, either by pushing the coring tool straight through the middle or by carefully cutting it out with a thin sharp knife. Make sure not to leave any seeds.

5. Place the apple(s) in the baking dish.

6. Layer the following into each apple: some of the raisins, some of the butter, then a bit of the cinnamon sugar. Pack each down a bit with a clean finger and repeat. Finish off with cinnamon sugar around the exposed part of the apple. Do not put raisins outside the apple as they will burn.

7. Pour a ¼ inch (1 cm) of juice into the bottom of the pan.

8. Bake uncovered 70 to 90 minutes. Serve with ice cream.

VARIATIONS:

Try the following instead of, or in addition to, the basic recipe: Dried cranberries, dried cherries, white raisins, maple syrup, brown sugar, ground cloves and nutmeg (only a little of these), or walnuts.

4. It takes apple trees four to five years to produce their first fruit. The apples may range from cherry size to ones as large as grapefruit.
5. There is no fat, sodium, or cholesterol in apples, though a medium apple has about 80 calories. Apples are also a good source of fiber and vitamin C, iron, and phosphates.
6. Modern doctors have discovered that apples can help reduce high cholesterol, soften gallstones, reduce fever, help prevent heart disease and cancer, and aid digestion.

SEVEN HILLS OF SWEET

Once in a lovely kingdom called Sweet, which was nestled among seven hills, there lived a noddy old king who loved chocolates. His father had loved gumdrops, his father's father had loved licorice, and his father's father's father—who had established the kingdom—had loved anything sweet. But this king loved chocolate above all else.

He had chocolate flakes for breakfast and chocolate sandwiches for lunch. He had chocolate burgers for dinner, which caused seventeen cooks and one dessert chef to quit over the years. He had his castle painted brown so the bricks would look like chocolate bars and poured hot chocolate into the moat. The moat dragons were so fat, they lay in the water like huge brown blimps.

Worst of all, the noddy old king had named his three sons Nougat, Toffee, and Cocoa—and his only daughter Fudge, That brought them great distress for they had always wanted to be named Tom, Dick, Harry, and Rosabella-Lynn.

This story is an original folktale by Jane Yolen, first published in Cricket Magazine in 1995.

There are three kinds of folktales: old stories transmitted mouth to ear over and over again; written-down tales taken from the folk tradition that—once written by a strong writer (Perrault, the Brothers Grimm, Disney and the like)—become the versions of a tale; and art tales, invented by a particular author, that look and sound like folk tales but are not.

Now one morning, when the king was down in the dungeon helping stir the latest vat of chocolate, the captain of the guard ran down the stairs crying, "Sire, sire, the kingdom has been invaded."

Well, the king was not as noddy as all that. He knew that chocolate was one thing, but war another. He ran up the stairs, straight to the royal war room. There he found his children and the wise men and women of the kingdom waiting for him.

"Who is invading us?" the king asked.

Fudge pointed out the window. Far away, like a brown stain on the seven hills, was an army standing at the entrance to the valley.

"Do we know them?" demanded the king.

"They have not given their names," replied Toffee.

"Nor the king they serve," added Nougat.

"Nor their reason for being here," said Cocoa.

"We must meet them without delay. Immediately. At once," cried Fudge. "We haven't got all day." It was not for nothing that she was called Fudge the Nudge.

So the king strapped on his armor, buckled on his sword, and girded up his loins. Then he was hoisted onto his battle horse and by noon was riding at the head of his army towards the invaders.

Toffee, Nougat, and Cocoa rode behind the king, but Fudge rode at his side, crying, "Hurry, Father. Turn left, turn right, straight ahead."

"Stop!" said the king.

The royal army stopped. They looked at the vast brown army that sat like a stopper in a bottle at the head of the mountain pass. The army went neither forward nor backward, neither up nor down, and overhead buzzed a hundred thousand flies.

"What a strange army," mused the king. He rode closer to see what he was dealing with. When he turned back to tell his daughter, she was gone, his sons were gone, and his army was gone as well.

Then the king turned to look again at the brown soldiers and saw that their chocolate hats were melting onto their chocolate heads and their chocolate heads were melting into their chocolate uniforms and their chocolate uniforms were running into their chocolate boots. Under the noonday sun, the entire army melted into a chocolate river that rushed toward king and horse, sweeping them away into the moat alongside one of the bloated moat dragons.

It took two winches to drag the king out and a dozen scrubbers to clean him up. And when they were done, the king called a conference with his sons and daughter and the wise men and women of the kingdom.

"It's one thing to love chocolate," the king said. "It's another to almost drown in it. I've had enough to last the rest of my life."

"Hurrah!" cried everyone.

Notable writers of original folktales are people like Hans Christian Andersen ("The Little Mermaid," "The Ugly Duckling," "The Nightingale The Princess and the Pea,") Oscar Wilde ("The Selfish Giant", "The Happy Prince,") Frank Stockton ("The Lady and the Tiger,") Madame LePrince de Beaumont ("Beauty and the Beast,") and Laurence Housman ("The Rat-Catcher's Daughter.") Many of their fairy stories were never meant for young readers.

Then the king turned to his children. "To remind us always of this change, I will give you four new names."

The three boys all winked at Fudge, because the chocolate army had been her idea after all. They knelt before their father and he held up his hands and proclaimed, "From now, my sons, your names will be Carrot, Tomato, and Cabbage. And you, my lovely daughter, will be Cauliflower."

"Cauliflower. . ." Fudge began. But as Cauliflower the Nudge is not a nickname that comes easily to the tongue, she said no more.

And believe it or not, that is how the kingdom became known as Salad and how it was ruled—after the noddy old king died—by good Queen Cauli, the Flower of the land. ⭐

Sweet Chocolate Mousse

The last chocolate you and your army will ever need. (Serves a family)

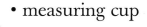 Equipment:

- measuring cup
- 2 bowls
- small saucepan
- mixing spoon or whisk
- electric mixer
- rubber spatula
- decorative glasses
- pastry bag and flower tip (optional)

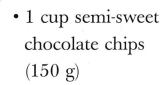 Ingredients:

- 1 cup semi-sweet chocolate chips (150 g)
- 3 cups heavy cream (690 ml)

DIRECTIONS:

1. Put chocolate chips in the first bowl.

2. Bring 1 cup (230 ml) of the cream to a boil, being very vigilant because cream will burn easily.

3. Pour cream over the chocolate chips and stir with a spoon or whisk until there are no lumps. Cover and refrigerate for 30 minutes to an hour.

Facts about chocolate:
1. Chocolate begins with the cacao bean, whose history starts back some 4,000 years ago in the Amazon region.
2. The bean's scientific name, Theobroma Cacao, means "food of the gods." The Mayans, who used cacao beans in the 6th century, called the cocoa tree cacahua-quchtl, from which the word cocoa comes.
3. Montezuma, emperor of the Aztecs, reportedly drank 50 goblets a day of a thick chocolate drink. The Aztecs did not have sugar to sweeten their chocolate drinks, but they used spices and even hot chili peppers.

4. When the chocolate mixture is cool, whip the remaining 2 cups (460 ml) of cream in the second bowl with the electric mixer until it stands up on its own. (This can also be done with a whisk.)

5. Beat the chocolate into the whipped cream, making sure to scrape down the sides of the bowl with the rubber spatula.

6. Using the pastry bag with the flower tip, pipe the chocolate mousse into decorative glasses or use a spoon to scoop it in.

7. Serve with whipped cream.

Whipped Cream:

Whip together 1 cup (230 ml) heavy or whipping cream, 1 tablespoon sugar and ½ teaspoon vanilla until the mixture is stiff.

VARIATIONS:

For more chocolatey mousse, use 2 cups (460 ml) of chocolate chips. Chill only for 30 minutes, or if longer, you may need to melt the chocolate mixture a little in the microwave before pouring it into the cream the second time. Try topping your mousse with berries. 🍎

4. Explorer Hernando Cortez brought back cacao beans to Spain, where they were used to make drinks that only the nobility were allowed to enjoy.
5. Today the oldest cocoa plantations are in Mexico, Venezuela, Ecuador, and Brazil.
6. Chocolate has high levels of certain chemicals that help the brain stay awake and alert.